1980

Brothers & Sisters/Sisters & Brothers

BROTHERS & SISTERS/ SISTERS & BROTHERS

Helene S. Arnstein

E.P. DUTTON / NEW YORK

Brothers & Sisters/Sisters & Brothers

For information contact: E.P. Dutton, 2 Park Avenue, New York, N.Y. 10016

Library of Congress Cataloging in Publication Data
Arnstein, Helene S.   Brothers & sisters/sisters & brothers.
Bibliography: p.   Includes index.   1.Brothers and sisters. I.Title.
BF723.S43A76 1979 155.4'43 79-14360   ISBN: 0-525-93059-0

Published simultaneously in Canada by Clarke, Irwin & Company Limited, Toronto and Vancouver

10 9 8 7 6 5 4 3 2 1   First Edition

To my husband, Bill—Because.

Contents

Acknowledgments

Fiction and drama, the Bible, and folklore have dealt with the subject of sibling relationships, but few nonfiction books have treated the subject as a whole. Accordingly, as soon as I embarked on this project and started my research, I began to realize the complex, multidimensional, and even global aspects of this undertaking. I consulted many persons, both lay and professional, and want once again to express my deepest gratitude to all of them for their invaluable assistance.

Scores of individuals told me of their present and past relationships with their sisters and brothers, their children, and other members of their families. Much of the information was obtained through interviews, correspondence, phone conversations, and informal discussions on planes, trains, or at social occasions, here and abroad. Other material comes from my own observations of sister and brother relationships over many years.

I want to thank my own brother, Arnold D. Solomon; my daughter and son, Nancy Wilson and Larry Arnstein, and Nancy's three children, Robert, age eleven; Sasha, nine; and Elizabeth, six. All of them have shown me the richness of sisterhood and brotherhood, the rewards of sibling devotion and kinship, and disagreement without hostility. My husband, Bill, ever patient and supportive, read first drafts of all the chapters, offering me constructive critical suggestions.

Special gratitude goes to Dr. Walter A. Stewart, instructor at the New York Psychoanalytic Institute and a member of the faculty at the Morristown Memorial Hospital in New Jersey, who so generously shared his wisdom, knowledge, and time with me as we discussed some difficult sections of the book. I am also deeply indebted to Dr. Peter Neubauer, director of the Child Development Center in New York City, and clinical professor of psychiatry, State University of New York, Downstate Medical Center, for giving of his precious time and expertise in helping me to clarify some knotty material. Grateful thanks also go to: Dr. Charles Feigelson, training analyst at the New York Psychoanalytic Institute; Dr. Herman Roiphe, clinical professor of psychiatry, Mount Sinai Medical School in New York City; and to Dr. Milton Viederman, clinical professor of psychiatry, New York Hospital-Cornell Medical Center, for granting me fruitful interviews.

Much appreciation also goes to others who gave me pertinent material from their professional experience. These are: Dr. Sylvia Brody, clinical psychologist and psychoanalyst, Center for Social Research, City University of New York; Ann W. Kliman, director, Situational Crisis Service, Center for Preventive Psychiatry, White Plains, New York, and Lucille Stein, C.S.W., therapist, faculty member of the Bank Street College of Education, and guidance counselor at the Ethical Culture School, both in New York City; Ada Daniels, M.S.W., of New York City, and Betsey Fox-Genovese, associate professor of history, University of Rochester, New York, read many chapters of this book and gave me helpful suggestions for which I am grateful.

Many thanks go to Katherine B. Wolpe, librarian at the Abraham A. Brill Library of the New York Psychoanalytic Institute, and Jeannette Taylor, assistant librarian, who gave me patient and constant help in tracking down important and much needed papers and books.

Last, but far from least, I am thankful to my good fortune in having had the skill of Jeannette Hopkins as editor of this book.

Prologue: Understanding the Past

Until recently, psychologists have given little attention to the subject of ongoing sister-sister, brother-brother, and sister-brother relationships. They have tended instead to examine in-depth nonkin relationships that have sexual content: premarital, extramarital, marital relationships, divorce, remarriage, etc., or the intergenerational relationships of mother-daughter, mother-son, father-daughter, father-son. When they have dealt with sibling relationships, they seldom go past childhood experiences.

But now there is a growing recognition among those studying the human psyche that it is high time to probe deeper into what the Bible, folklore, novels, and drama have long revealed, that adult sibling relationships can be intense, loving, hating, rewarding, and necessary.

In this day of constant self-questioning, where alienation, isolation, and detachment blight many people's lives, a rediscovery of lateral relationships that supplement the parent-child linkage is desperately needed. Parent and child are not enough. Sisterhood, brotherhood are in the process of rediscovery. The process is extending beyond the family itself to the larger human family. To be a "sister" or to be a "brother" now means friend and ally. Many adults with brothers and sisters have begun to reexamine these connections in their own personal lives. How can they become genuine sisters and brothers? Take the middle-age man who bitterly comments about a brother, two years his junior, "We haven't been on speaking terms for over six years. I don't even know how it all happened."

Three widowed sisters until their deaths at a ripe old age were still waging the competitive battles that started out in childhood. Each sought to show the others that *she* was the smartest, most accomplished, successful, and loved—constantly bragging to them of her most recent conquests and triumphs, and later, those of her children and grandchildren. How could this miserable state of affairs ever have taken place or continued so long?

Others have worked through their childhood sibling competition during the growing years so that by adulthood they are free to enjoy each other as *adults.* Three brothers, now in their midthirties and with families of their own, often reminisce affectionately about the fights and jealousies of their childhood. They are "there" when needed during rough times. They are brothers in the best sense of that word.

The key to transforming the natural rivalry of childhood into a creative friendship of adulthood is trying to understand childhood feelings, how and why they existed, and then, in the light of that, understanding, rethinking old resentments, abandoning these burdens, and rediscovering each other's true worth. George Santayana once said, "Those who cannot remember the past are condemned to repeat it."[1] Also, those who cannot *understand* the past are condemned to repeat it. Once that understanding is gained, we may be able to change the future.

The Roots of Jealousy and Rivalry

No one is spared pangs of jealousy, envy, resentment, and hate. These strong and bitter feelings shared by mankind have their roots in earliest childhood. Freud observed many years ago, "There is probably no nursery without violent conflicts between the inhabitants, activated by rivalry for the love of parents, competition for possessions shared by them all, even for the actual space in the room they occupy. Such hostility is directed against the older as well as against the younger brothers and sisters."[2] Bringing things up-to-date, with apologies to Freud, and "competition" and fights over the "space" they occupy in the family car!

Unhappy feelings that sprout in the nursery *can* haunt and plague us for the rest of our lives. That is, unless we received help from those close to us in handling these emotions in childhood, or unless as adults we can come to handle them for ourselves. Even hurtful put-downs, or arguments in adulthood over money and property are usually no more than updated versions or carry-overs of childhood contests.

Much of adult sibling conflict is based on what seemed to us in childhood the ultimate prize in life—to be the one and only in the eyes and hearts of our parents.

Psychologist Dr. Robert W. White of Harvard University has written in *The Enterprise of Living* about patients who sometimes were able to understand that they were still competing with their adult siblings "for the favor of parents who might be aged, senile, or even dead." These same patients began to recognize the fact that rivalries and competitions with people in their work or professional lives stirred up bitter and anxious feelings way out of proportion to the actual circumstances. These overly strong reactions—"legacies of competition in the family circle," as White puts it—prevented them from seeing things clearly and what the actual circumstances were in their present lives.[3]

A lab technician says he wishes he could work alone in the laboratory. He complains that his colleague, older by three years and with three years' more experience, "is always breathing down my neck. He nags and finds fault with everything I do. I get so nervous that I make even more mistakes.

It's just like it was with my older brother." But this man is not his brother. Why can't he free himself from his childhood bondage to his sibling?

A magazine editor recalls a painful experience whose origins were in childhood. "I was terribly angry and over-wrought when a younger, recently hired editor on the maga-zine was promoted before I was," this young woman told me. "The incident shook me so much that for weeks I couldn't sleep at night, and I soon realized that I was in need of psychological help. While in therapy I was able to see more clearly the reasons for my torment, hurt, and anger. My boss, the managing editor, had singled out Isabel, this attractive, ambitious fledgling editor soon after she was hired. I felt very jealous and resentful because my boss—a father figure to me —was someone I wanted to please, desperately. When Isabel received her promotion I felt altogether rejected by him.

"I later discovered that my rival, younger than I, had vaguely reminded me of my younger sister, Cynthia. Isabel's hair was curly like Cynthia's and she also had her winning ways—all of which I envied. I realized too, that Cynthia had always been Dad's favorite daughter, and strangely, my boss' attitudes and mannerisms reminded me of my father. I could see now, that in a way, an early drama in my life was being replayed all over again. Here was my boss, pushing me aside to favor Isabel, just as my father had pushed me aside for Cynthia."

Subsequently, this editor revealed, the tensions she had felt in the office seemed to subside when her anxiety ebbed after therapy. Had it all been a tempest in a teapot, she wondered? Now, freed to a great extent of her conflict, she was able to put her mind to work and concentrate again. Soon, she, too, received a promotion.

Adults' reactions to others and their treatment of them —good or bad—are a consequence, in large part, of the child-hood lived with growing sisters and brothers, learned through fights and tears, through laughter and the fun of sharing. The way we got help in dealing with our mixed emotions as children has made for the difference in our adult responses.

Within the safe shelter of the home we practice the skill of dealing with people, that is, of getting along. Despite our differences and squabbles, if all goes well we eventually learn to be more tolerant of each other, and are able to live in peaceful coexistence, at least. In the home we are helped— or not helped—to learn when to stand up for our rights and when to give in, when to take and when to give—and how to win a few, lose a few, without gloating in victory or sulking in defeat.

Some homes exude warmth and acceptance as well as friendliness and welcome to outsiders. In other homes the atmosphere is cool, no one expresses emotions openly, there is no closeness, and everyone seems to go her or his own way. The siblings usually absorb these different attitudes. A young group of adult sisters and their brother, living out West, none yet married, and lacking the funds to travel across the country to attend the family Thanksgiving, elected instead to get together for themselves for the occasion at one of their own homes, each of them partaking in some of the preparations as they always had. But another set of siblings, two sisters and a brother, couldn't care less when they see each other or their families and have almost lost contact.

New Sibling Relationships that Supplant the Old

The cliché that "people never change" is nonsense. When they are willing and *ready* to change in attitudes and actions, most people can change. That is, they can if they are able to achieve a better understanding of the roots and growth of their sister and brother relationships and how these relationships might have gone awry. These insights should go a long way toward enabling a grown sister and brother to accept the advantages of shared memories, similar beginnings, and those unique bonds that can and often make sister-sister, brother-brother, and sister-brother adult relationships among the most rewarding of human friendships. To reach out toward the other in an effort to revitalize an ailing relationship is to risk rebuff, but the risk is far less than the potential for gain. How comforting to know that siblings —even those living far away—can be counted on when the going is rough, and that the frightening feelings of loneliness and detachment that often pervade our lives in a troubled, uneasy time can be eased by a newly discovered sister, a newfound brother.

I

SIBLING RIVALRY, SIBLING LOVE

1
Problems of
Favoritism

Wilma, a graduate student, one of two sisters and a brother, remembers her shock when at the age of ten she overheard her father declare proudly to a visiting friend, "My favorite child, Sarah, made this ashtray for me."

Then there is the successful Chicago businessman who confessed that he still winces when he thinks of the way in which his widowed mother introduced him and his older brother whenever they were together, "This is my son, Dr. Harris, and that's Frank."

Favoritism often leads to lifelong difficulties—if not outright hatred—between brothers and sisters. Obvious favoritism, preferential treatment of one child over another, cuts deep, especially in a small family where the competition for the love of a parent is keen. In larger families, the edge of the pain may be somewhat softened by other compensations. Brothers and sisters often offer each other consolation, and give and receive loving substitute parenting, since someone is always helping another down the line.

The Pain of Rejection

The pain, of course, is that bitter sense of knowing that you are less well thought of, less worthy than another in the beloved parent's eye—no matter how hard you try. It is that

9

miserable feeling of being rejected. Even if the parent isn't
aware of feeling or showing favoritism, the feeling of inferiority suffered by the disfavored one is often carried over into
adult experiences leading to fear, or expectation of, rejection. An adult who has had this childhood experience may
unconsciously invite rejection, convinced she or he is un-
worthy.

The pain can also cause havoc among sisters and brothers during their growing years, sometimes contributing to
bitter estrangements in adulthood.

Cain slew his younger brother Abel in a fit of jealous rage
because Jehovah—Father of all—preferred Abel and, therefore his offering of sheep, and spurned Cain's gift of fruit and
grain without any word of appreciation for his efforts. Handsome, precocious Joseph was envied and despised by his
many older brothers because he was the most cherished son
of their father, Jacob. When Jacob gave Joseph a special gar-
ment—the famous coat of many colors—the brothers plotted
to kill him and, relenting, nevertheless sold him into slavery.

A 1948 novel by Anne Meredith, called *The Sisters,* presented Janet, an unusually plain child who was a disappointment to her parents. Eight years later, Cassie, another
daughter, was born. This child from infancy on was exquisite;
her charm captured the hearts of everyone. " 'Now, my dear
Marguerite, you have produced something worthy of you,'
Mrs. Amberley's friends congratulated her." Of course, poor
Janet became accustomed to being compared to her sister to
whose spell she, also, succumbed. In the prologue of this
dramatic novel of more than thirty years ago, Janet cries out
in her anguish, "It was always Cassie—Cassie who had beauty
and grace for whom nothing was too good. Cassie must be
painted, Cassie must be photographed . . . Cassie must have
pretty clothes."[1]

One of the most dramatic illustrations of bitter jealousy
evoked by marked parental favoritism occurs in a scene to-

ward the end of *Long Day's Journey into Night,* Eugene O'Neill's tragic, semiautobiographical play. Jamie, the hard-drinking, "ne-er-do-well" elder son, lashes out venomously in a drunken fury at his consumptive younger brother, Edmund, though, in some odd way, he loves him. "But don't get the wrong idea, Kid. I love you more than I hate you." But his jealousy is more powerful than this love, and he says, at the end of an earlier diatribe, "Mama and Papa are right. I've been rotten bad influence. And worst of it is, I did it on purpose." He goes on, "Did it on purpose to make a bum of you. . . . Never wanted you succeed and make me look even worse by comparison. Wanted you to fail. Always jealous of you. Mama's baby, Papa's pet!"[2]

Some parents deny that they have any favorite and sincerely believe they "love" all of their children equally, although their real feelings are betrayed by their behavior. Barbara Silverstone and Helen Kandel Hyman write on this point in their book, *You and Your Aging Parents:*

"Look, ma, no hands!" a triumphant four-year-old may shout, balancing for the first time in his life on a two-wheel bicycle. If his mother's response to this dramatic accomplishment is merely, "Be careful! Don't scratch your brother's bike!" this four-year-old may wonder what further act of bravery he will have to perform in order to gain the maternal spotlight. He may keep on trying all his life, hoping that one day he will do something to make his mother's face light up for him the way it does for his brother. Like eager scouts, less-favored sons and daughters more often push themselves through life to do more and more good deeds hoping for that just reward. But sad to say, no Brownie points are given out to middle-aged daughters and no Merit Badges to graying sons.[3]

There is another kind of favoritism, which, when obvious, can also have devastating effects on the siblings. And that is when one child may be preferred by the mother and another by the father.

An industrial psychologist, engaged as a consultant to a

large furniture manufacturing company, told me that after the owner of this company and his wife died, the rivalry of his two sons for their parents' love continued. One son had been his father's favorite, an athletic, forceful individual. The other, four years younger, handsome and creative, had been his mother's favorite. Within a short time after the brothers took over the business, their rivalry for their parents' favor came into sharp focus. At times they acted as they had as children, vying for the affection of the other parent, through trying to placate some of the executives—currying their favor as if they were their parents. Soon the brothers were not on speaking terms. When board meetings were held, one brother would express an opinion and ask an officer of the company to relay it to the other brother. When one brother entered the office of any executive to discuss a point, the other would be sure to follow after his sibling had left, asking, "What did my brother say to you?" This competitiveness, this lack of trust, and the climate of suspicion it engendered so reflected on the profits of the business that things gradually slid from bad to worse and the corporation went bankrupt.

The Burden of Being Favorite

An obvious singling out of a child by a parent, a difference in the quality of treatment, isn't necessarily rewarding for the favored child. Neither this child nor the disfavored child can help but be affected by the parents' attitudes. Marked favoritism, may, in some ways, have strengthened that preferred child's self-confidence; still, favoritism can exact a heavy price. The preferred brother or sister may try to lord it over the others, becoming the object of their justified resentment. Or, the favored sister or brother may carry a burden of guilt, because down deep that child, now adult, understands that the partiality from which she or he benefited was unfair. Leo, a college student, told me that his father had always stood up for him in his arguments and fights with his older brother, even when he was in the wrong. "Pop kept giving me compliments, but rarely praised Joey, who tried so hard to please him. I lived with an awful sense of guilt and injustice. But Joey and I talked things over long ago when we were kids and whatever envy he has, it has not interfered with our relationship. But he sure hates Pop." Leo is now studying law and intends to become a criminal defense lawyer. Who knows whether the direction of his life was changed by his dislike of injustice?

Guilt may also have made a sister (or brother) feel beholden, obligated in some way to less-favored siblings. The chosen one may also feel she is beholden to, and must follow, the demands of her parent—an emotional blackmail of sorts —that is, if she wants to keep her coveted place. Cordelia, in Shakespeare's play, wouldn't play this game. King Lear expected and asked her, as his favorite child, to outdo her sisters in their declarations of love for him—insincere as they were. Cordelia loved her father dearly, but she believed love was its own proof. She refused to justify her love for him in words, thereby losing her place in his heart as well as her inheritance.

Dependence upon parental favoritism can cripple and bind the favored. A mother of three daughters told her eldest in childhood that she was the "best" (best-behaved) and most loved of all. The favored girl felt compelled by this praise to sacrifice her individuality. In trying to "set an example" of good behavior to the others—as her mother bade her—she was obliged constantly to hide her anger so that she wouldn't forfeit her favored position. To make up for her guilty knowledge of being best-loved, she became a virtual slave to her sisters. They, in turn, sensing her guilt, exploited her for all it was worth in childhood and in adult life.

Favoritism in Reverse: The Black Sheep

José Quintero, the stage director known for his superb staging and directing of O'Neill's plays, was not only drawn intensely to these dramas, but found that O'Neill's conflicted and often anguished life paralleled his own in many ways. For an article written for *The New York Times Magazine,* he told Barbara Gelb, "From birth on I was branded a disaster." Quintero's father had not only been terribly disappointed at his birth because he wasn't the long-awaited girl—there already were two other sons—but ashamed because his son's skin was quite dark, unlike that of "his upper-class Panamanian family." But, more, his two elder brothers were good students at school, well behaved and tidy, whereas "Quintero disliked most of his subjects and often came home from school with his clothes ink-stained."

Half-forgotten, half-buried resentments from childhood can rise to the surface and spill over in adulthood. As Gelb describes it:

> "When I was growing up," [Quintero] says, "my birthdays were never celebrated the way my brothers' and my sister's were. I was always being punished." Once, during a particularly bitter period [as an adult], he gave himself a birthday party at the terraced apartment in New York where he was living. He got himself quietly and ferociously drunk and as each guest arrived bearing a gift, he slipped out to the terrace and hurled the unopened gift over the side.[4]

Out of fear of losing the parent's love, often a favored sibling avoids a close relationship with the black sheep, the one who didn't "fit in" with the family traditions and expectations. The rejected child may then be filled with self-hate —accepting the opinion of the family, regardless of its accuracy. Psychiatrist Walter A. Stewart, instructor at the New York Psychoanalytic Institute, observes that, "the other children may also hope secretly that all the bad things they feel about themselves can be safely projected onto this scape-goat."

A young woman professional wrote me from the West of the many trials she had suffered as a youngster. She had been fat and homely, and envied her two older sisters and brother who constantly teased her about her weight. She ate even more to compensate for her lack of love and recognition. Their mother was distant, and their father, a doctor, ul-traconservative and strict. At fourteen, she ran away from home, was picked up by the police and put in jail.

"As a lesson to me my parents let me rot there for two days—I shudder to even think about it." Later, she joined the antiwar movement. Her parents were so upset, "they nearly disowned me." Shortly thereafter her father died of a heart attack and her sisters and brothers accused her of having "broken his heart." She knew this was unjust because he'd had heart disease for many years. "But can you imagine how I felt?" Over the years she began to see why they harassed her. They, too, had been pressured by the parents. She was, as she wrote to me, "a perfect, defenseless scapegoat." She moved away. Now when they see each other "the time I spend is too precious to waste on negative emotions."

Dr. Stewart says, however, that sometimes one of the children—most always a sister—rescues the denigrated child, perhaps out of a strong maternal and protective in-stinct, or because by helping this brother, she can prove to her parents, the father in particular, that her brother is wor-thy.[5]

Parental Identification with One Child

Identifying with one child, having a special psychologi-cal rapport should not be confused with favoritism, or *prefer-ring* one child and showing partiality.

Mothers and fathers have been known to disfavor a son

or daughter because unconsciously that child represented a part of themselves that as children they hated and rejected or that their own parents hated in them. Or, they were angered by a child who had the guts to talk back to them and, at the same time, unconsciously envied that child for having had the courage they lacked.

Almost every parent has, secretly or openly, been entranced with, or singled out one of the children—for a day, a week, or during a particularly gratifying stage of his or her development—in preference to another child who is going through a stretch of puzzling or irritating behavior. One child may be more restful, fun, or altogether easier to handle. Maybe a mother found herself more in harmony with a daughter whose disposition matched her own, which may have been placid, assertive, or whatever. Or that mother may have found more delight in her outgoing, active, daring child with traits she admired and did not have. An intellectual father may enjoy the child who follows his own tendencies or interests. In Saul Bellow's book, *Humboldt's Gift,* Charlie, a brilliant scholar, finds himself drawn closer to one of his two daughters, the one who seems more like him. He begins to dream about the future, "For I have plans for Mary. Oh nothing as definite as plans, perhaps. I have an idea that I may be able to provide the child's mind with my spirit so that she will take up the work I am getting too old or too weak or too silly to continue."[6] Yet another father may have gotten a tremendous boot out of being the father of an athletically talented child, precisely because *he* had always failed at athletics.

Sisters and brothers may be loved *differently*—albeit equally. The late Wyatt Cooper, actor, writer, and editor, was well aware that he identified more with his elder son, but he seemed to have handled it in such a sensitive way that each boy could feel his individual place with his father, and know that his father cared. He wrote about these relationships in his book, *Families,* explaining that each of his sons delighted him in different but equal ways. "Carter and I recognized ourselves in each other from the very beginning. We think alike and often read each other's thoughts, communicating with glances and half-smiles without the necessity of words."

He had a separate but equal relationship with his younger son, Anderson, who used to say to him almost every evening, and right after dinner, " 'Let's go to the pizza place,' not because he was hungry for a slice of pizza, but because those jaunts were something between the two of us. It gave him a chance to talk about whatever was on his mind, but more than that, it was an opportunity for one-to-one man-to-man contact without having to share the connection with an older brother who'd managed to get there first."[7]

Perhaps the most endearing illustration of a father and his sons comes from a California architect, one of five brothers, all of whom have remained on the best of terms. He loves to tell the story of how his father replied to the question, "Which of your sons is your favorite?" "Dad winked and said, 'I have five fingers on my hand. Each one of them is equally important to me!' "

Sex Preferences

"Isn't it just marvelous!" exclaimed a group of women working together in a fund-raising campaign, "Kathy's first child is a *boy!*"

The women's movement has done much to change that ancient and still living tradition, which puts a premium on the birth of a male child, but proud fathers still distribute cigars to all and sundry when that first son is born. Women rightly feel that these attitudes can make their imprint on a female child early in life, causing a girl to feel put down—a scarring experience for her sense of femaleness and individual value.

A director of a coeducational camp for children tells me

how embittered she had been by her relationship with her mother who preferred her brother, three years her junior. "Our relationship—mother's and mine—was ruined by what I perceived as a strong favoritism to my brother due to his sex. Of course there were other factors; he was an adorable child and easy to manage. I can still remember the many many times when my mother heard the sound of our childish squabbles from another room. She never bothered to find out what was going on, but would just yell, 'Anna, stop!' The light in my mother's eyes as she pointed to my brother and said, 'This is my son!' affected my feelings of self-worth. I felt that by being a girl I was a second-class child. My father and I were more compatible, but during the early years he wasn't around as much as my mother whose imprint was firmly made. Although his love helped, it didn't quite eradicate my lack of belief in myself."

Everyone who has had children or who plans to have them may recognize in themselves a fairly universal ten-dency. Most of us want to extend ourselves in our children and live once again through them, hoping to give them a better deal than we had. Or, if our childhood was happy, we want them to recapture this good life. A mother lives somewhat through her daughter, and a father lives through his son.

What if that longed-for daughter or son doesn't arrive? What if the next child, or next, or even further children are of the same sex? You may have been that last same-sex child who disappointed your parents. Yet if your parents quickly recovered from their first let-down and set these frustrations aside to love you, you suffered no injury. Not all are so lucky.

A famous actress, at the pinnacle of her career, told a reporter during an interview, "My father was so angry and disappointed when I was born—a third daughter instead of a son—that he left home in a temper and didn't return for several hours."

The story of his angry flight, told to the little girl early in life, became a family legend. Her father's initial rejection —as represented by the legend—so damaged her self-image that she drove herself frantically and relentlessly in her chosen career to capture her father's notice and acceptance of her worth. But even the great success she finally achieved, and the public's adulation of her talent, beauty, and charm never seemed to bring her satisfaction or self-assurance. She trembled before each performance as if it would be the last chance to succeed in her life. Underneath her self-doubts lay the feeling that no matter what she ever did she could never make it up to her father for having been born the wrong gender. She could never receive the recognition and love she craved from him, which her envied sisters received without any effort.

When parenting isn't all it should be—and even when it is—one of the older brothers and sisters may step in and take on a nurturing parent role and become a model and guide for the sibling, as well as a source of warmth, protection, and love. Simone de Beauvoir was the firstborn and cherished child. But, in *Memoirs of a Dutiful Daughter*, she writes of her parents' disappointment at the birth of a second daughter instead of a son: ". . . it is perhaps not altogether without significance that her cradle was the center of neglectful comment." She gives a touching portrayal of her sister's plight in being the younger same-sex daughter:

Relegated to a secondary position, the "little one" felt almost superfluous. I was a new experience for my parents: my sister found it much more difficult to surprise and astonish them; I had never been compared with anyone: she was always being compared with me . . . whatever Poupette might do, and however well she might do it, the passing of time and the sublimations of the legend all contributed to the idea that I had done everything much better. No amount of effort or achievement was sufficient to break through that impenetrable barrier. The victim of some obscure curse, she was hurt and perplexed, and often in the evening she would sit crying on her little chair. . . .[8]

False Perceptions of Favoritism

Sometimes, children and adults mistakenly believe they are disfavored. Adult sisters and brothers have exclaimed to each other, "But I always thought *you* were Mother's [or Father's] favorite!" As one mother, a warm and perceptive personnel director in a large accounting firm, put it to me, "You just can't win! Ted, our eldest son, was a very serious, plodding, introverted boy who had difficulty in expressing both his needs or feelings, whereas Bob, our younger son, was cheerful and outgoing, enchanting everyone with his appealing ways. I bent over backwards to help Ted along with his problems and devoted much time to him. To my dismay, just a few weeks ago—and the boys are now twenty-eight and twenty-five, each with his own apartment—Bob said to me as we were talking about the past, that he had always felt I loved Ted more because of the extra attention I had given him. I was just flabbergasted! His father and I decided it was time for a 'fireside chat' and got the family together. I laid it all out on the table, then everyone had his say, and the discussion that followed was marvelous. I think that now my boys know the score. Maybe I'm being defensive, but I am sure that down deep Bob felt he was just as much loved as his older brother because they've always gotten along so well."

Brothers and sisters may resent each other for years because of a discrepancy between their *perception* of where they stood in their parents' affections, and the *reality*. There are a number of "reasons" for such distortions of the true facts. Some of us are so sensitive that if anyone in a small group is telling a story and looks at the others in the group but doesn't glance in our direction often enough—or even at all—we are convinced that he likes the others better, or maybe he has something against us and is showing it by this silent insult, this covert rejection. The fact may well be that

the tense and self-conscious storyteller is so absorbed in getting his tale across that he is just able to focus his eyes on
those in the range closest to him, and hasn't the foggiest idea
of whom he is or isn't looking at. Children's feelings are
sometimes even more vulnerable and prey to distortion.
Younger children sometimes see the greater freedom and
privileges accorded an older sister or brother as added evidence that their mother and father prefers that child. This is
because the very young are not yet able to understand that
greater responsibilities go along with greater freedom, and
that love and privileges are not necessarily related.

Parents may have handled a shy and sensitive child more
carefully and tenderly—as did the personnel director—than
they might a more boisterous, seemingly self-sufficient
youngster, who, in youthful insecurity, could have mistaken
this difference in handling for preferential treatment. A father may have used a different tone in talking with his daughter from the tone used with his son. Certain activities and
special occasions, such as the games of a young football
player, or the recitals of a musical child, call for excited
praise. A brother or sister's quieter exploits, such as stamp
collecting, may provide few opportunities for enthusiastic
admiration. The stamp collector may well feel less important
or less loved than the more publicly praised sister or brother,
though each is equally loved.

A pediatrician tells of her sister, Irene, who was born
prematurely and who "was in very delicate health for many
years. My mother and father hovered over her and protected
her from many longed-for experiences. Because Irene received so much solitude, I always felt that *she* was the favorite and resented her bitterly. And Irene felt that our parents
were deliberately sabotaging her development, letting me
have all the advantages and exciting experiences such as
skiing and skating and staying overnight with friends, be-

cause they loved *me* more! It wasn't till years later that we could talk out our misconceptions and resentments and feel better about our sisterhood."

Getting Over Memories of Favoritism

What sister or brother was always treated equally, absolutely impartially at all times? What growing sisters and brothers didn't feel resentful and envious of the other sib whose needs at the moment called for special attention and care while their own needs were neglected for a time? Many sisters and brothers remember only the bad moments and not the good ones. But many forgot or took for granted that they came in for their share of attention once the trouble or crisis was over. This was a part of life and growing up. On the other hand, obvious favoritism for a brother or sister, preferential and even differential treatment that leads to rejection, is not easily forgiven and never forgotten. It is a chilling and demolishing childhood experience and it erodes adult self-confidence unless we intervene to prevent it.

Although we cannot and should not attempt to be psychoanalysts and try to probe into the depths of our psyches unaided, it may help to know something about the unfinished business of childhood. For the angers and half-forgotten resentments from the past can be ignited into flames by the slightest word.

Once we begin to understand more about the source of certain feelings and attitudes, we become able to handle them with more ease and success. Our feelings will not disappear miraculously, but sometimes our negative emotions and attitudes *do* change gradually without conscious awareness; that is, when we are ready and willing to alter these emotions and attitudes. When adult brothers or sisters become aware of how these past experiences and untoward attitudes on the part of elders can have hurt another sibling, or even themselves, the simmering anger and resentment between them may be reduced and the mutual snipings lessened. In discovering that childhood insecurities about where we stood in our parents' affections—real or imagined—may have been mutually upsetting and not the "fault" of that sister or brother, we may find that an adult relationship will begin to replace the childhood one.

2

Finding Identity Despite Individual Comparisons

An electrical engineer, now twenty-nine, who has moved far away from his parents and siblings, puts it this way: "It still resounds in my ears—that parental voice nagging, 'Why can't you have good manners like Eric? Why can't your room be neat like Stanley's? Why can't you bring home good marks like Ella?' I always felt dogged by failure after these reproaches and began to hate my brothers and sister for making me feel that I couldn't match them in any way."

Some parents who love their children equally and have no favorites nevertheless from time to time pit one child against the other.

Sincerely believing they are stimulating their children to "improve," oblivious of the fact that there might be adverse effects on the relationship among their children, many mothers and fathers praise one child at the expense of another, or compare one sibling detrimentally to the other.

Who wants to be told that she or he is less attractive, intelligent, charming, successful than someone else? And who likes to be compared unfavorably to another sister or brother?

There is nothing quite as painful to us, as children, nothing so undermining to our sense of adequacy or that makes us feel so resentful toward our brothers and sisters as to be told we are wanting in comparison to another brother or sister.

Sometimes this parental attitude backfires, and the extolled child becomes a pain in the neck to Mama or Papa at some later stage.

"When we were growing up," says Avery, a mother of two, and assistant buyer in a large New York City department store, "Mother tried to play each of us against the other. I was ten when I first began to notice what was going on. I happened to have been a quiet, serious child, buried most of the time in books." Avery's mother would often take her aside and tell her what an exceptionally good and lovable child she was, what pleasure she gave her, etc. At first Avery was delighted to know that her mother thought her such a paragon of virtue. "But then," Avery declares, "she'd lambaste Paula, my older sister by four years. She'd tear her to pieces—her friends were awful, her clothes a sight, she was 'fresh' to her and wouldn't obey—and add, 'Paula is just killing me!' But when I turned thirteen and began to strike out for my independence, the tables were turned. She'd take Paula aside and tell her what a disappointment I was, how selfish, inconsiderate, and that she always knew she would be proud of her Paula!" Soon the two sisters realized that their mother was a cool manipulator, wanting to break up their closeness—of which she was jealous—by trying to divide and conquer them. "It didn't work!" Avery concludes.

Labeling

Stories are endless about families with daughters in which beauty was rated as priority number one, and the sister who fell below average in this attribute felt through her very pores that she wasn't living up to family standards—even if no words were ever spoken about it.

Before the women's movement got under way many families were still placing little value or emphasis on their daughters' business or intellectual achievements. A girl who was considered "plain" was pitied because she stood little chance of finding a "catch"—a "suitable husband"—unless she was quite well-to-do. The cult of beauty still dominates despite the women's movement.

In other families intellectual capacity and performance are emphasized, and beauty almost frowned upon. In one such family there were four daughters. One of them, as brilliant as her sisters, was beautiful in face and figure. Unknown to her family, she entered a beauty contest. When they found out, her sisters and parents considered this almost scandalous behavior—especially since she had won. Countless sisters will admit that one of them was praised as the brilliant one of the family and the other as the beauty, until one day, to their great surprise, "I found out that I also had 'brains,'" or "I discovered ways of fixing myself up so that people commented on my looks too."

Can sisters and brothers ever forget that they were referred to as "the scatterbrain," "the slowpoke," "the dependable one," "the brawn," or just "the kid"? Sometimes sibs feel as if those labels had been attached to them with epoxy glue, and even after they become totally different adults, the hated labels adhere. "Let's go see what 'the brawn' is up to," says a man to his wife as he is about to phone his younger brother, now a college professor. "What do you suppose 'slowpoke' has to say about this?" asks a young mother. ("Slowpoke" is now a top woman politician.) It can be threatening to see how different—and better—a sibling has become. It means we have to construct a totally new and realistic image of this sister or brother, which is hard to do. And, therefore, we cling to old images.

Labels are not always meant as a form of nasty teasing but may be repeated out of habit, or out of a wish to extract some of the past closeness of the family from that mixed bag of happy and unhappy memories.

But things don't always work out this way, and more often the results of labeling are damaging to the growing personality.

Many adult brothers and sisters recall that one of them was complimented at times for being so reliable, another for having acted so intelligently over some matter, or chastised for having been so absentminded, or whatever. So far, so good. But when these sibs were rigidly tagged or labeled, they may have felt not only an unconscious obligation to carry out those assigned roles ("the scatterbrain"), but often they made this parental image of themselves the basis for their own self-image. Some psychiatrists call this "the personal myth" that we all weave about ourselves to some extent. Others refer to it as "reflected self-appraisals" or even a "self-fulfilling prophecy."

"If it's always been impressed on you that you're the intellectual member of the family," a librarian told me, "then you feel you have to live up to this expectation, and you may begin to resent, envy, or even hate your sister or brother who has other options open."

A popular football player says it wasn't until after he had given up professional football that he discovered through vocational aptitude testing that he also had brains. He never had been given a chance to develop his mind, only his muscles. At nine he already was being pushed into athletics because he showed exceptional skill; his parents let him neglect his studies.

Says a much sought-after piano coach, "I felt disqualified from taking piano lessons as a child because my family said my sister was the talented one. Dad said, 'Walter, don't even waste your time trying.' I'd play by ear, and finally drummed up enough courage to say I'd take lessons even if I had to work after school to manage them." The young man majored in music in college, went on to a music conservatory and now is head of the music department at an eastern university—

taking only accomplished pianists as pupils. "It was years before I forgave my sister whom I envied for getting the lessons I didn't dare plead for for such a long time, believing she was the talented one. But now my sister is a textile designer and we can laugh at our former agonies. It wasn't till much later that I discovered she didn't *want* those lessons despite her 'talent.' We would never stereotype our own kids. We would praise and encourage any unique talents or interests they displayed, even if one of them was similar to that of another sibling."

Comparisons with Parents' Own Siblings

A number of the problems that afflict many grown brothers and sisters were actually inherited from their parents, who in turn were heir to these problems from their parents. Mothers and fathers often unconsciously act out their own sibling dramas on their children, casting them into a role of a once or still adored (or hated) brother or sister. Words or actions of their child may ignite memories of mistreatment they received from a sister or brother in their own childhood.

"Perhaps I'm rough on Betty when she uses that condescending tone of voice in talking to Dick, telling him to do this or that," says a father who describes how he severely reprimanded his eleven-year-old daughter when she corrected her younger brother. "But I so vividly remember the way Jane [his eldest sister] used to boss me around when I was Dick's age. It still makes me livid to think of it. I won't let him be pushed around like that." Actually, Dick was less perturbed than his father. He was well able to hold his own and tell his sister firmly to "lay off" when she annoyed him. The father was unable to recognize that his strong response to his own childhood experience was distorting his view of a contemporary reality.

A psychiatrist briefly outlines a case in which a mother cast her son, age twelve, into the role of her own much-despised brother. Her brother Rod was two years her senior, and she claimed he "always got away with murder at home." As a child he was frequently ill, "and mother pampered him then. He had the whole family coming and going. He could twist everyone around his little finger," she declared angrily. "I often had to make his bed because he was too lazy to do it for himself, and Mother insisted that I carry out that chore for him." Rodney had refused to attend college because he wouldn't apply himself and disliked discipline and routine. Selma feared that her son would turn out just like Rod, "because, I guess, he's inherited it; it's in the family."

"Actually," the psychiatrist interprets, "without any awareness on her part, Selma was pushing her son into a position like her brother's. Whenever Tom showed any undisciplined behavior, Selma saw red and overreacted because of her experience with Rod, whom she had actually envied and resented. How come, she thought, Tom can always lie around and be a slob just like Rod while I have to work my fingers to the bone? As a result of her pent-up angry and jealous feelings about her own brother, she was blocked from being able to help her son work out his very real problems. He received criticism and orders, but no help. Tom had two choices: to be blindly obedient, or defiant, like his Uncle Rodney."

Attitudes may be passed down from one generation to the next unless the cycle is broken through new insights or professional help.

Learning to Live with Our Differences

"My brother Ned was tall and slim and could run fast as a streak," says an amiable buyer for a bookstore. "I was short and inclined to be heavy. I minded this terribly as soon as I got to the age where I could compare myself to him, and others my own age. But my parents—and also Ned, because he absorbed Ma and Pa's attitudes—didn't put any importance on this difference. Mother and Father told me that everyone is either tall or short, plumpish or thinnish, or blond or brunette, or has this or that talent. Someone has to be one way or the other. 'What really counts,' they said, 'is what kind of a *person* you are and how you can adapt to your characteristics. Sure, if you're short and want to be on the basketball team, forget it. But there are no size requirements for being President of the United States—or for being loved!' I couldn't ever forget their words, and I felt it over and over again in the way they all treated me. It so happened that I did most of my growing while at college."

"Liz and I were always envious of something that would be considered as quite unimportant today—our individual type of hair. But Mom made it all important on account of her strong beliefs of how she thought we should look," a mother who runs charity drives as a volunteer remarks. "Liz had beautiful, abundant, tight brown curls that even bounced. My own hair, blond, very fine, hung straight and limp—like cooked spaghetti. I remember Mother putting my hair in paper crimpers every night when I was about four, but as soon as my hair was combed out the next day, each curl collapsed again. Later, during our adolescent years the styles changed and Liz envied me because straight hair was 'in.' Mother was heartbroken when Liz had her hair thinned out and straightened. Now, it's the other way again and at the moment curly hair is the fashion. But it matters not to us, and we do recall with some humor and some annoyance at how we always were being compared by Mother on matters so very superficial."

Each human being comes into this world with his or her own innate personality. One child is more sensitive, anxious; another, tougher, and more resilient to life's pressures. Laura has great charm; Susie seems quiet and shy. Each child also inherits various endowments, traits, talents, and other potentialities that may or may not be unearthed. And everyone is born into a different family environment because of his or her ordinal position; the health and mental health, and happiness, of his or her family at the time; the family's social or economic standing; or even a parent's revised view of child-rearing. One can safely say—except about identical twins—that no two children come out of the same mold. No human clones have yet been born! Yet all too often one sibling feels the need to be a carbon copy of the other. During their school years, as sisters and brothers begin to develop their sense of "Who am I?", Gregg notices that his eyes are blue like Mommy's, but Brother Joe's are green like Dad's. Maybe he'd like to have it the other way around. One boy may be chubby, growing east and west, as many youngsters do preceding adolescence—somewhat like the book buyer and his brother Ned—while his older brother is referred to as "that long drink of water." A woman remembers how dismayed her elder sister was, because, at twelve, no traces of approaching puberty were in evidence, while she, the younger girl, was already sprouting breasts.

As children assess these differences, and others already mentioned, unfortunately they have no way of realizing that those differences rarely remain permanent. Those disparities —particularly in looks and scholastic achievement—are open-ended, because in the course of growing up, and even after, people often change.

Some of us had parents who came to the rescue and helped us tap the resources of our individual strengths and assets, stimulating and encouraging each of us to pursue a particular bent. Maybe we were helped to choose an uncontested area in which we could shine, or maybe we were informed that it was okay to enjoy the similar interest of a sibling—or even develop the same talent. What about those musical families in which each plays an instrument and a chamber music ensemble or popular rock band results?

One would have to dig deeper to discover the motives

that have stimulated countless numbers of brothers and sisters to choose similar careers. It may be competitiveness, similar talent, interests, background, or family expectations that they would follow some tradition. It is worth mentioning just a few famous same-career sibs: Kennedy, Rockefeller, Marx, Mayo, Menninger, the two brothers Grimm of our fairy tales, and the "BeeGees" rock singers—three brothers, Barry, Robin, and Maurice Gibb; brothers and sisters Warren Beatty and Shirley MacLaine, Peter and Jane Fonda, and Fred and Adele Astaire; two brothers and one sister, John, Lionel, and Ethel Barrymore; two sisters, Dorothy and Lillian Gish, Lynn and Vanessa Redgrave; and three sisters, Ann, Emily, and Charlotte Brontë.

A city planner still remembers how his mother bailed him out during what for him was a trying moment. "While Mother was being congratulated because of Eileen's outstanding talent as a dancer, she noticed me, evidently standing close by and shifting uncomfortably from foot to foot. She quickly caught the signals and rescued me with a swift, 'Yes, it's wonderful, we are so proud of Eileen. But someday you must come over and look at Nick's collection of seashells and see how he has mounted and cataloged them. He's got the makings of a museum curator.' "

During adolescence, when hormonal and physical changes occur, along with new inner drives and consequent physical unrest, young sisters and brothers are even more vulnerable to the comparisons they feel impelled to make between themselves and another sib. Even if it was far from so, many teen-agers have seen themselves as ugly, clumsy, stupid, and ineffective in comparison to a sister or brother.

Dr. Norman Kiell, professor at the Brooklyn College Psychiatric Services Center, expresses this inconsistency in *Adolescence in Fiction:*

He may dislike his brother because the latter is better-looking, brighter or stupid or unattractive. He may like a popular brother because of reflected glory, but he might also prefer an unpopular one because no one would make invidious [to him] comparisons. He would like to be an only child because of the advantages that might bring, but he might also want brothers and sisters to secure greater anonymity and privacy.[1]

Of course, these ambivalent feelings are part of the adolescent girl's life, too.

Wherever the sisters' and brothers' differences add to their *parents'* pleasure, it must add to their own pleasure. Each is then able to recognize the fact that she or he is also a "somebody." Whether or not we are in the same profession or pursuit shared by a sister or brother, the more we can feel a "somebody" in our own right, the more at ease we are likely to be with ourselves and with each other.

3
Competition and Rivalry

"From birth," writes Joan Fontaine of her bitter relationship with her sister, Olivia de Haviland, "we were not encouraged by our parents or nurses to be anything but rivals, and our careers only emphasized the situation. As both Olivia and I can be classified as achievers, our impetus may well be the sibling rivalry that still exists."

Rivalry can be a prod to achievement. It can also corrode pride in achievement. Joan Fontaine tells of the 1941 Oscar award presentations, when the names of five nominees for the best actress of the year were read. Joan's name was among the five. But when she heard her name called as a winner of the Academy Award, she froze in her chair. Her older sister, Olivia de Haviland, was sitting at a table directly opposite her. " 'Get up there, get up there,' she whispered commandingly. Now what had I done! All the animus we'd felt toward each other as children, the hair-pullings, the savage wrestling matches, the time Olivia fractured my collarbone, all came rushing back in kaleidoscopic imagery. My paralysis was total. I felt Olivia would spring across the table and grab me by the hair. I felt age four, being confronted by my older sister. Damn it, I'd incurred her wrath again!" Joan admits that Olivia took the situation with grace, especially since she had barely missed winning the award the previous year.

Five years later Olivia finally won her own Oscar. Joan went over to congratulate her sister. "She took one look at me, ignored my outstretched hand, clutched her Oscar to her bosom, and wheeled away. . . ." Rebuffed, Joan retreated to the privacy of an empty theater box until the ceremonies were completed.[1]

Other stories of competition seem pale in comparison to the vignette told by Fontaine about this bitter rivalry, which began in the nursery and continued on and on. But these tales have their significance, too. One of them demonstrates how the rivalry of the past—even if only mild—can survive the years. An eighty-eight-year-old woman, living in Warsaw, who had suffered extreme poverty and personal tragedy, heard through her niece that her sister, age ninety, had died. Yet the first and only comment the old lady made when her niece, the sister's daughter, came from America to visit her, was, "Did Annie's hair get all snowy white like mine?" The petty rivalry of childhood had survived.

Pressures to Succeed

"It was years before people stopped saying, 'That's Cathy M's sister!' " a charming interior decorator who has found her own place in life, confessed to me. "My sister is a well-known opera singer. When we were growing up, Mother's ambition to have Cathy succeed and become famous through her golden voice and 'make Mother proud' was relentless. She also tried to push me into the public eye as a figure skater at which I excelled. Father just kept his distance and said little. He was a rather withdrawn person and scared of Mother. I never reached anything near my sister's success in a field which didn't appeal to me that much anyhow. When I was successful at a skating contest, she lavished her 'love' on me. Cathy and I, therefore, became intense rivals fighting for Mother's conditional love. It wasn't until Mother's death when she was fifty that Cathy and I got a chance to discover each other's inner selves, to find out how we felt about our childhood, our careers, and our trials. We had been so busy before trying to be 'best.' Now, in our own families, 'competition' is a dirty word."

Clearly, something within these two sisters rebelled against their mother's emotional blackmailing, and, finally, through the crisis of their mother's death, they became reconciled.

Everyone cherishes hopes and dreams for their offspring and enjoys vicarious as well as real pleasure as their children progress through their own lives. But sometimes parents' personal ambitions or emotional lives have been so empty and stunted that their children become their major compensations; they often cling to the children, living their own lives through them. Their children may serve—unconsciously—as instruments to gain for them the glories they never could capture themselves. They try to mold their children's personalities according to their own specifications. Unless the children rebel, this tight control is usually accomplished at great expense to their children's own emotional lives, needs, and desires. Under such conditions, sisters and brothers are often pitted against each other as they succeed or fail to bring their parents the rewards they seek.

The children of such parents often fail to develop humane values of warmth, compassion, tenderness, sharing, and acceptance; they may become as competitive as Madison Avenue ad executives, cosmetic sales managers, or supermarket entrepreneurs. Since early childhood these sisters and brothers got the message that approval (love) is allotted only for successful performance. If she or he was "best" it meant being best loved by Mommy and Daddy. The child often grew up into an adult who believed that mother and father—and then the world—give love to the one who is "best" and too bad for the loser.

Three sons of driving, ambitious parents were told when

they brought home their school report cards: "Oh, you got 85 percent; why couldn't you have gotten 90 percent?" And when that son, or another, received 90 percent, the parents would complain, "But why wasn't it 100 percent?" It was always the boy who could top his brother in accomplishments who received, for the time being, all the warm embraces, attention, and accolades from his mother and father —while the other two boys were pretty much ignored. As the boys grew older, their rivalry increased and they constantly bickered, making disparaging remarks about and to each other. Although all three became successful businessmen, none could ever enjoy either his own success or that of his brothers.

Once in a while you hear of a brother or sister who has made it in the world of finance or high society and who is ashamed of the siblings he left behind. A social worker told me she remembers a boy who had come to her settlement house many years ago chiefly to play basketball. "He was handsome and brilliant, but had a ruthless driving quality in his play that made some of us shudder. We knew through sources that his father constantly pushed and drove him. 'Leo,' he would say, 'you're always to come out on top; don't let anyone keep you down.' Leo received one scholarship after the other, and following graduation from an Ivy League college, he went on to the Harvard Business School. Not long after, we heard he married a Boston society girl—by that time having made a fortune through real estate. A sister later told us the most he ever did for his family was to send a joint check to them yearly, with a note reading, 'To cover all your birthdays, love, Leo.'"

The social worker ended this story by saying, "We all were sure that there may have been some kindness in his gesture. But we were even more certain that the money was sent basically as a guilty payoff for his avoidance of contact with his family whose presence would have revealed his background, and, as he probably thought, threaten his present status."

But, many people protest, we live in a competitive world. How are young people going to meet it if they aren't urged to win, to come out first, to grab all the prizes?

Everyone has within him or her—as part of the human condition—a desire to achieve, to excel, to master, and even to outshine others. Just watch the expressions of joy, glee, and triumph as a baby first pulls himself or herself up, takes those first steps, says that first word. From early childhood on, rivalry and competition can no more be avoided than the common cold. Life, itself, in communist, fascist, socialist, or capitalist countries alike, stimulates and encourages this urge. Those whose natural competitive spirit is totally undermined may become fearful of asserting themselves, or be unprepared in maturity to deal with the outside world.

A Long Island school superintendent declares that "striving to be number one at home or in the outside world can be innocently aggravated by seemingly innocuous games such as giving children stars for excellence to paste on the bulletin board. When one of us brushed our teeth, made our bed without being reminded, handed in the best report card, went to bed on time, etc., for a month, thereby receiving the most stars, we were given a present or money. All of this just fed into the normal competitive feelings of the winner and added to the loser's competitive envy and hostility, that I can assure you."

"In our family," reports a management consultant, "surpassing others was not viewed as all that important. Although Mom and Dad didn't hide their joy when one of us came home with good marks, they didn't let us feel it was a disaster if we failed. Mind you, our childhood wasn't always a picnic, and like all families ours had its problems too. But I always will remember how Dad tried to get us involved in many games that depended more on luck than on skill, such as Parchesi, dominoes, or simple card games. He showed us—and really believed it—that there was a great deal of enjoyment in tennis, baseball, etc., games requiring practice and skill, but that one could enjoy a game, too, without winning. You know, 'the game's the thing' attitude. We didn't really buy that attitude until we got to be a bit older, since I do recall crying once because Tom, my older brother, always beat me at checkers. Edwina, too, would stalk off in angry frustration, while Alice just shrugged her shoulders and gave up resignedly. Dad would say to all of us at such times, 'Look, Allie, Ed, and Harold, Tom's had more experience and knows the game better. You'll catch up in time and I'll show you more moves.' And he'd do it. Most of all our parents both understood that it is an undeniable wish and natural thrill of everyone to win, and they didn't make fun of us when we were downhearted after losing. But they did make us all feel that we wouldn't be gaining or losing their love or respect by either winning or losing, and encouraged us to join group athletics where the team more than the individual counts."

Sibling One-Upmanship

Many brothers and sisters, however, are still trying, unconsciously, to settle some score of years ago, or are still playing the game of one-upmanship. Some may have become the "successful" members of the family—if we are talking in terms of financial, social, or career prominence—but they may not feel all that successful in the deepest reaches of their mind. Having carried over from childhood a lack of self-respect and self-esteem—having grave doubts about their true worth—they may still need to prove their superiority by lording it over another brother or sister, or by acting unkindly or condescendingly toward them.

In *Families*, Wyatt Cooper reminisces about those days in childhood when he used to cross swords with his younger brother, Harry. Cooper had been so jealous of this younger sibling, he explains, that "my purpose was to discredit him. It was not enough that I be considered of good character; his must be shown as disgraceful." He had told his own two sons about these early events and of his hurtful attitudes, which he later regretted: for instance, how he'd disparage his younger brother by remarking to him condescendingly that he guessed Harry wasn't doing long division, yet, when obviously the boy wasn't up to it.

Cooper comments that his sons are aware of the parallels in their own relationship and that of his and Harry's early relationship. This fact has become a sort of joke among the three of them. "Carter has the impulse to do to Anderson exactly the kind of thing I have described my doing to Harry, but the difference is that both of them will recognize what is happening and they can laugh about it. Carter will start to say something that asserts his superiority, all meekness and sweet interest: 'Anderson, are you still on your first reader?' Then he will catch my eye, grin sheepishly and say, 'I know, just like you did to Harry.' "[2]

Since parental approval means more to a child than anything else in the world, Carter well understood that his father disapproved of his actions. Telling his son with humor how he had rejected such behavior in himself gave the boys a valuable lesson in human relations: Try not to put another person down. Competition is one thing. Injuring a sister or brother is another.

Envy of somebody—especially a brother or sister—who does something better, or who seems to be more esteemed by others, is part of human imperfection. It is common and there is nothing "wrong" with feeling this way. However, when an attempt is made to criticize or downgrade the envied one, the results can injure both parties. In any case, the attempt to play one-upmanship against the envied sibling through denigrating some shortcoming is an empty victory.

Whatever satisfaction is gained from a momentary squelch is outweighed by guilt because those who have the slightest love for a brother or sister are likely to feel remorse over hurting their sibling.

4

Fighting, Teasing, and Solutions

Psychologists Dr. Brian Sutton-Smith and Dr. B. G. Rosenberg, authors of *The Sibling*, asked several large groups of fifth and sixth graders from two-children families, "How do you get your sibling to do what you want him (her) to do?" and "How does your sibling get you to do what he (she) wants you to do?" From their answers, the investigators compiled a list of forty different strategies. The results were tabulated according to the eight possible combinations in two-sib families: older brother on younger sister, younger sister on older brother, older sister on younger sister, etc. Here—not in order of preference or frequency—is what the children said they did to get their way with each other:

Beat up, belt, hit; Promise; Boss (say do it, shut up); Scratch, punch, pull hair, bite; Bribe, blackmail; Ask, request; Tickle; Flatter; Ask to do something because older (younger, a boy or a girl); Wrestle, sit on, chase; Bargain; Ask parent for help; Get angry (shout, scream, yell, get mad); Play trick; Complain to parent; Cry, pout, sulk; Take turns; Tell tales; Attack things (hide toys, spoil bed); Explain, reason, persuade; Ask other children for help; Break things (toys, let air out of tires); Do something for the person; Ask for sympathy; Take things (ride bicycle, steal toys); Make feel guilty; Bother (turn off radio, change TV channel); Pretend to be sick; Use prayer; Tease (name calling, pester, nag); Threaten to hurt; Be stubborn, refuse to move; Threaten to tell; Make a wish about it; Stop from using phone, bathroom, toys; Spook them; Exclude (can't play, can't go with—lock out of room); Give things (candy, money, toys); Give their choice (watch TV, play); Be nice, sweet talk.[1]

Mind boggling! No member of the junior Mafia, or battlefield strategist could think up more ways of manipulating or controlling others. And while this childhood song is ended its melody lingers on. These early tactics of persuasion are often continued into adulthood.

The following scene was told me by a cousin who attended a family gathering that included two sisters and a brother, all in their early forties. An argument broke out over some trivial matter. Accusations were flung back and forth. "You haven't changed a *bit,* Helen; you were always *pigheaded* as a child and everyone had to give into you!" "Sure, and *you* got your way by *yelling* and out-shouting the rest of us just as you're trying to do now!" "Look here Tony, if you think you're going to make us feel *guilty*—using your historic 'holier than thou' attitude—you've got another think coming!"

Power Struggles through Punches and Pummelings

"My next older brother, Jonathan, three years my senior, used to beat the pulp out of me when I was a kid, and it continued until he was a junior at high school when he lost interest," a novelist remarked. "Maybe I brought on some of the fights at times, but I doubt whether I'll ever forget the humiliation and anger I felt at always being vanquished in these combats because I was smaller and weaker. My books are filled with themes of vengeance."

Brothers and sisters who were on friendly terms in childhood most of the time can't even recall their wrangling episodes, which they vaguely remember came and went like summer storms. But others remember incidents of constant friction that continued almost into adulthood.

How did our families feel about physical aggression? Did they ignore, sanction, or forbid it? Was our childhood fighting intense, frequent, or occasional? The pattern of our memory of childhood battles can mar our adult lives and govern our relationships with our boss, fellow workers, spouse, and with our own children.

Marcus [middle child] managed to enrage Konstantin [eldest] by flapping at him with his muddy towel: Konstantin hit Marcus, Christopher [papa] hit Konstantin for hitting Marcus, Rose [mama] shouted at Christopher for hitting Konstantin, and then at Maria [youngest] for smiling so smugly because the two other children were in trouble.

How familiar is this little scene drawn by Margaret Drabble in *The Needle's Eye*.[2] And how many parents are driven to distraction by the seemingly endless bickering, by the shouts of outrage, and by the furious given-and-taken-blows by their children.

Quarreling, whining, pushing, wrestling, hairpulling, kicking, and some pummeling are common in most homes with children. Yet even the most heated physical encounters that appear to be heading toward fratricide often end amicably and are fast forgotten. But what causes these angry clashes?

Outlets for Anger

Anger triggers aggressive responses to such unhappy experiences as: feeling put down, humiliated, frustrated, disappointed, rejected, afraid, threatened, jealous, insecure, physically attacked, abused, powerless, or any of a number of assaults on who and what we are. Young children may have temper tantrums in response to any of these provocations, and kick or lash out in body language. Their brothers and sisters are a natural object to vent their feelings upon—less dangerous than attacking the powerful parent.

As brothers and sisters continue subsurface struggles to find their place in the family pecking order, and for the exclusive attention and love of mother and father, younger children may also want to prove their power to their older sib, while the older ones seek to protect their own interests and the rights and dignity of their seniority. When these vital interests clash, as they are bound to, quarreling breaks out. Skirmishes may ensue over the slightest provocation, "She took my eraser!" "He pulled my hair!" "He pushed me!" "She's pestering me; she won't leave me alone!" "He turned off my TV program!" It is a familiar litany.

Like working adults, youngsters who are cooped up with one another day in and day out, with no choice in the matter of their company, cannot help but get on each other's nerves at times, as well as in each other's way. When things become heated enough, feelings boil over and sisters and brothers may strike out at the person they feel is making them miserable. Little by little, in the process of becoming civilized by loving, understanding parents, they learn to control their angry *actions,* though perhaps not feelings, initially to please their mother and father and retain their love, later to fulfill their own ideals. However, they might still slug, kick, scratch, or bite the older or younger sibling when threatened because their controls aren't yet well developed. But, in time, as children mature they learn or should learn to recognize and accept anger as a universal human feeling.

Physical responses are transferred to inanimate objects —a ball to kick, a pillow to punch, a door to slam. For both young and old, football, basketball, hockey, and other competitive sports give both participants and onlookers a healthy and acceptable outlet for normal feelings of competitiveness and hostility.

Real or imagined gripes begin to be expressed verbally rather than physically. Freud pointed out, quoting an unknown English writer, "The man who first flung a word of abuse at his enemy instead of a spear was the founder of civilization."[3] Rage and anger is then expressed through arguing, swearing, sulking, and name-calling.

Teasing and Verbal Assault

"Betty still drives me crazy with the sarcasm she directs at me," June, a computer programmer, complains about her older sister, a married advertising executive. "But I can never tell *her* off. She used to tease me and make fun of me even in childhood. The only thing I could say then, meekly, was 'Sticks and stones will break my bones but names will never hurt me.' But the words *did* hurt and I felt thoroughly demolished." Childhood habits can control adult relationships.

In Owen Wister's classic, *The Virginian,* Trampas, no friend of the hero, calls him a son-of-a-bitch, whereupon the Virginian draws his pistol and demands an apology, saying, "When you call me that, smile!" The narrator, who had heard the Virginian accept the same epithet from a friend, perceived that this was an example of the old truth, that the letter means nothing until the spirit gives it life.[4] That is, teasing may be acceptable; a verbal assault is not.

School-age and even older sisters and brothers often address each other with endearments such as, "You jerk (dummy, stupe, dope, rat fink—and more)!" Strangely, this kind of taunting or kidding may have rung out with tones of genuine warmth and affection, even pride. Frequently, it is a way of establishing contact, of reaching out toward the other, covering up the embarrassment or self-consciousness engendered at times by giving or receiving direct blandishments. When said good-humoredly, "C'mon over here, dopey, and help me with these fractions," and "Okay, dumbo, wait until I've finished this page," it may be just a part of the give-and-take of the young, and understood by them as such.

At other times, especially if teasing is chronic, the tones and undertones in these same words may resound with the intention of cutting the sibling down to size—the kind of derogation to which that child is most vulnerable. At a time when a sister or brother is failing at school, "dumbo" or "dopey" can be cruel. If an overweight sister or brother is called "fatso," "jumbo," or "pudding face," or a short one, "half-pint," "shortie," or "shrimp," the teasing may reflect a need to put the other down, and thus to pull the teaser up. The putting down makes the teaser feel superior—temporarily—just as certain drugs can give a person who is feeling low a high, before its effect wears off. The teasers in such melees may have been suffering from jealousy of a sib's other attributes or lovability, or from a general feeling of being less appreciated or loved. The tensions may also have been caused by problems outside of the home. In either case, sisters and brothers sometimes need a scapegoat upon whom they can vent their tensions and angers. Needless to say, adults *or* children with a good sense of self-value don't need to downgrade another to upgrade themselves.

Jessica Mitford, the fifth of six sisters and a brother, writes, in *A Fine Old Conflict,* of the teasing among her sisters, the techniques of which "were perfected by sister after sister and passed down the line." She found that being a younger sister of Nancy was a particularly "toughening experience" since Nancy had "an uncanny ability to ferret out one's weak spots, to be exploited in unmerciful teasing." The bitter taste of those childhood and adolescent years stayed with her. Strong feelings cropped up during an interview with a writer for the London *Observer,* who was doing an article on sisters. "Since there were so many sisters in our family, she wanted a comment from me; she had already spoken to Nancy in Versailles, who had said, 'Sisters stand between one and life's cruel circumstances.' I was startled into saying that to me, sisters—and especially Nancy—*were* life's cruel circumstances. . . . "⁵

Persistent, malicious, and deflating teasing is actually a form of angry aggression. In adulthood it often reappears in the form of biting sarcasm. And many sarcastic, brittle remarks aimed at a brother and sister mark scorn, another defense against feelings of fear, envy, or self-doubt. (A comedian or humorist can make us laugh because his sarcasm or scornful cracks are directed at universal foibles. Since he is not deriding us personally, we can see the humor in our weaknesses without feeling personally attacked.)

As with the brother or sister who always seems to incite to riot, the chronic teaser is often the sibling who may have felt unfavorably compared to the others, overly jealous of their attributes, inadequate as a person, left out, or maybe bullied at school. The knowledge that the aggressor may have been an unhappy sister or brother in childhood may help to decrease whatever grudges or hostility still remains between them in adulthood. A psychological verity that few would dispute, says, in effect: The more each child in a family receives love, respect for his or her dignity, and an appreciation of that child's individual self, the less uncontrollable this growing person's need is to knock down or undercut older or younger brothers and sisters, and other people, as well.

Fighting Back

What about the sister or brother who cringes and never has the courage to fight back?

Afraid to express rage, some children—and adults—run away from it, and feel helpless in their hurt. June, the computer programmer who could never "tell off" the sister who made caustic remarks to her, revealed that she had always felt crushed whenever anyone kidded her; all of her defense reactions were paralyzed. She was so tongue-tied that she couldn't "answer back." Actually she was bottling up her rage, and one day it might explode in her sister's face.

Some sensitive and self-effacing children never gather the courage to fight back because they sense that any physical retaliation, even in defense, is disapproved of and that they'd be more loved by appearing submissive and defenseless. "Because it looked as if I'd be the fall guy at home in my childhood," says a young physics instructor at a New England boarding school, "my father stepped in and said it was okay to defend myself when Brad went after me. He said, 'Don't submit to abuse, yet don't feel challenged to a duel every time your brother taunts or provokes you. Walk away and ignore the challenge—unless this challenge persists unrelentingly.' "

And what can an adult sister or brother do when a sibling becomes a thorn in the flesh by constant attempts to deflate, provoke, or whatever?

Had June told her sister off by releasing her long pent-up anger at last, it might have done her some good and shocked her sister—for the time being. But it is unlikely that matters between the two would have improved. Unless the relationship itself actually changes, the hostile pattern will simply be repeated. For some, it is possible to say to the offending sibling words that imply, "Let's sit down and talk things over; let us not have hard feelings, but rather try to understand and accept our differences and shortcomings." It is only through searching communication that we can break down those barriers that cause such misunderstanding and loneliness.

Provocateurs and Diplomats

"My mother says it was useless to find out 'who started it,' " a father of four young children comments. "She tells me that I, the younger boy, would often say with an innocent look on my face, 'But Hank hit me *first!*' Often it *was* the

younger one who provoked the older child into retaliation—
as with Marcus and Konstantin—thereby appearing as the
victim, attracting sympathy, and hoping his older brother
would "get his."

No one wants to see a child in the family physically
injured, humiliated—whether younger or older—in a nasty
fight. Children's dignity and feelings as well as their bodies
are injured by a sibling's ferocious onslaught. Even the attacking sisters or brothers may have suffered remorse and
experienced guilt for whatever harm they might have done.

"That will teach you not to hit your little brother again!"
one father used to shout as he spanked his elder son. But it
never did. This father was a provocateur. The hostilities may
have ceased for the moment, the truce usually lasting until
Pop (or Mom) was out of sight or out of the house, and then
open warfare began again. Besides, the boy wasn't being
"taught" anything except that "might makes right," because
his bigger, stronger father was actually saying one thing and
doing another. (A paper presented at a meeting of the American Psychological Association had the title, "If You Don't
Stop Hitting Your Sister, I'm Going to Beat Your Brains
Out!"[6])

Because a brother probably identified with the angry,
attacking side of his parent at such moments, he'd often
continue to let out his physical expressions of anger on a
smaller, more helpless sibling as an opportunity to even the
score. Since parental hitting represented approval of one
child and disapproval of another, it may have stimulated
further animosity between the contending brothers. And because violence compounds violence, such boys often have
been among the brutalizers: the bullies, the wife-beaters, and
child abusers. Girls treated with brutality often repeat the
violence on their own children.

"Mother was the greatest diplomat of all," says the head
of volunteers in a large city hospital of a much wiser parent.

"Whenever Milly and I got into nasty tussles, she would quietly but firmly lead us into separate rooms and tell us to stay there until we both could be 'civilized' again. Of course we both felt 'misunderstood' and soon after, we found each other again. We began to notice, while making up, some admirable qualities in each other we had never discovered before!"

Sometimes when children are bored they'll indulge in horseplay that can easily deteriorate; one of the partners receives an unexpected stunning blow and a free-for-all commences. Another sister, who has been close to her brother since childhood, tells me this about their early spats. "Whenever we were bored or tired, clouds would burst and we'd pull hair, scratch, wrestle, or pummel. After settling us down with a glass of milk and a cookie, or getting one of us to set the table earlier, or go on an errand, Mom, or Dad if he happened to be there, would say something like this, 'We know you get mad at each other and it's okay to feel that way, but you can *talk* out your angers. That makes the difference between human beings and animals. Find a language for your feelings and *listen* to each other so you can settle your differences in a reasonable, workable way. Fighting makes life unpleasant for everyone. Physical force and vengeful acts don't solve or prove anything, any more than wars do.' We were always deeply impressed by the philosophy behind these words and never forgot them."

Sibs love and they hate. In childhood they bicker, tease, provoke, fight—and make up. With sensitive awareness and understanding on the part of their parents or parent, most sibs manage, gradually, not to tread on each other's toes, but rather to juggle their own needs for status in the family with those of their sisters and brothers. This can be achieved only as each of the siblings begins to feel sure of her or his special place and identity within the family. With growing self-esteem—basic to esteeming others—they no longer need to take out their feelings of self-doubt and inadequacy on their sibs.

As brothers and sisters develop that sense of "I"—meaning, "I'm loved just because I'm me"—they tend to develop a sense of "we" and "us" as a family. They may then discover, despite angers, the special benefits of just being and having siblings—and in time, reach a sense of family unity that survives.

5

Alliances and Cooperation

Brothers and sisters may be rivals, even enemies at times, yet they are also capable of being unselfish, mutually cooperative, generous, and loyal to one other. Adult sisters and brothers frequently tell how they loaned each other money, clothes, equipment, or, how, as children, they agreed to trade chores in good spirit. "I was fourteen," says a father of two, "when I occasionally asked my younger brother, Tom, if he'd do the dishes for me so I could get to club meetings. I promised him that I would help him with his homework the following evening in exchange for his kindness. Tom would agree without a murmur." He continues, "You can imagine how pleased I was then to observe Pat, my ten-year-old daughter, generously offering her younger sister, Liz, her bike, suggesting, 'Liz, it's high time you got the hang of it. Just take it whenever I'm not using it.' "

Unless bitter animosities have driven brothers and sisters apart, many help to cushion the emotional as well as physical blows the other receives from the outside world. A sister's or brother's disappointments are often taken to heart, even if it wasn't always acknowledged openly. "If *anyone* should have been given the lead in the school play, it was *Lucy!*" a teen-age sister declares with emotion, recalling how she felt her sister's disappointment as her own—giving evidence of how brothers and sisters tend to become emotionally involved and identified with each other. One may have cheered wildly for the others during an athletic contest, or, with great pride, outclapped the audience at a school musical performance of a sister or brother. These are the brothers and sisters, relatively secure about themselves in relation to parental affection, who may continue to show such pride way into adulthood. It is not infrequent for an adult to be content to bask in a sibling's glory: "Yes, that's *my* brother (or sister)!"

The Sibling Mafia

In this sibling underworld the motto often is "All for one, one for all." "I had an older brother who became my champion at an early age," a young New York musician remembers. "Nicky would plead in behalf of me, 'C'mon, Mom. Get off Arty's back. All the other guys in his class are wearing long hair; it's the style.'" Many adults must recall how they ganged up against their parents to protect a much picked-on sister or brother, or persuaded them to grant her or him a privilege they felt was justified. Some youngsters pass on valuable information to the others, like a dental hygienist who warned her younger brother, "Don't ask for that baseball mitt this evening, Wally. Dad is in a *foul* mood and he is sure to say no." In one family observed by psychologists Dr. Stephen Bank and Dr. Michael Kahn, whenever the alcoholic father become abusive to the older brother, his sister would suggest that she and her brother play cards, get out of the house, or go for a walk.[1]

To share secrets with a sister or brother was to feel superior to Mom and Dad, who couldn't possibly know what *they* knew. The horseplay, the whispers, and giggles at night were part of the game. And pillow fights may have ripped the pillows apart but they bound the youngsters closer together, especially after a parental bawling out.

Three grown sisters and their two brothers have often

laughed over the pranks they played on each other and on their parents in childhood. "We'd make pie-beds when the other least expected it, and once we hid Sidney's notebook when he was late in getting ready to meet the school bus. Of course, we gave it right back to him on the bus. One evening Milly placed a frog on Allan's pillow just as he was about to get into bed. And I loved to tell fibs about my parents' being royalty who had left me here for adoption, so I wasn't really their sister after all! One night three of us hid all the family silver and ornaments. We awakened Mom and Pop in the middle of the night telling them we heard noises in the house and were sure that robbers had broken in. When they saw all the ornaments missing as well as the flat silver, they were terribly excited and were about to call the police, but then we confessed. Although *we* thought it was funny, they didn't think it was funny at all!"

Brothers and sisters may threaten to spill the beans, but unless very young and not yet able to use judgment and reason about such matters, sibs are more apt to observe their own version of *Omerta,* the inviolable Mafia pledge of silence. Tattling has deeper causes and meanings, some of which may be revenge for past insults, a result of an already growing feud, or severe jealousy. It is a short-range retaliation prompting further conflict. ("I never forgave my brother for ratting on me," a bartender at a hotel in Boston recalls. "I had cheated on my algebra test and the little skunk had found out and told Pa. I got what for!")

In homes where children are accustomed to authoritarian forms of child-rearing, should a mother or father thunder, "*Who* did it?", the *Omerta* may hold even more firmly since no sib is likely to tell on the other. An innocent one may even take the blame. The respect and opinion of the junior Mafia group counts heavily. As sisters and brothers grow up, the often unspoken commitments between them serve to strengthen their emotional ties.

One of three sisters says, "We know each other inside out, we are on the phone daily, telling each other things we couldn't possibly share with outsiders. We are like best friends but with an added plus; we know that anything we tell the other won't go any further. Even so," she added with a slight laugh, "at times I wish my sisters didn't know about some of the things I did in the past—of which they're only too glad to remind me—because I'd like to forget them."

Sisters and brothers often keep each other in line, listen to how the others think about things, to what they say. They teach, judge, and groom one another for the outside world.

Sociologists James Bossard and Eleanor Boll show how children were disciplined by each other in large families. They write in *The Large Family System:*

> One time when the youngest sister was to have dinner ready and she hadn't even started the meal, the next two proceeded to prepare the dinner and talked about her all the time she was hiding behind a door and heard the unkind things they were saying about her. She never did let it happen again.

They also point out that if one of the children didn't do his or her share of work, that child would be left behind while the others went off to fish, swim, skate, and play.[2]

When they become adults, some brothers and sisters (and other relatives at times) build up a protective wall around themselves—no matter what dissensions, resentments, and bitterness may exist behind that wall. They may present a picture to the world of a close-knit harmonious group. In the words of one such family member, "Even though Ella with her phony airs and uptight Tim are big pains in the ass a good deal of the time—and I'm sure they have their own thoughts about me—in the long run we'd stick together through thick and thin. We might even hate each other, but we'd never let the family down." And while they may criticize or judge one another in no uncertain terms, should others make derogatory remarks about anyone in the family, they will hotly defend her or him no matter how right the criticism. They close ranks.

Two sisters, radical in their youth, had both been members of the Communist party. It was their family and their life. Then the younger sister was expelled from the party for an act of defiance. Her former friends passed by on the other side of the street. But her sister and brother-in-law quit the party in loyalty and burned their communist books. Sisterhood was more important than politics.

Although sisters and brothers often take things from each other, such as rudeness, criticism, domination, neglect, etc., they would never take from a friend, there is a tendency in this most paradoxical of all relationships to grow to cherish the past. One sister of a younger brother and an older sister sums up that feeling. "As you get older, you become less critical of others; you begin to accept them or at least try to ignore their faults. You also become more accepting of your sisters and brothers, and you aren't too bothered by, let us say, their lack of tact. You no longer cringe in embarrassment over one's sibling's loud voice or another's stinginess in tipping waiters and cab drivers. And even though the past hasn't been so perfect, you don't want to let go of that common history which is so deeply embedded within you."

In childhood, sometimes it's a matter of, "If you can't lick 'em, join 'em." Brothers or sisters may decide to team up together, and parents can encourage cooperative efforts. One mother told me of her own two boys, "Gil, eight, and Howy, ten, who scrapped constantly like little puppies, decided while we were gone for the weekend that our bookshelves needed rearranging. To my mother-sitter's horror, they got a ladder and took down each volume, deciding that the books should be arranged by length and width. The project took longer than anticipated, and when we showed up, countless books were scattered all over the floor. Aghast, but touched by our boys' joint endeavor, we praised them for their united effort, knowing that the rivalrous aspects of their relationship were considerably reduced through this enterprise. Insisting that the remaining books be put back, we didn't rearrange the others for several months by which time the boys were into new mutual enterprises. Today they are partners in a literary agency."

Sisters and brothers who spend time with friends their own age have an easier time. "When we got together again, we appreciated each other more," a brother of five older and younger sisters and brothers remembers. Ralph Schoenstein, the humorist, writes in *Yes, My Darling Daughters,* "The girls have always loved each other so profoundly that when Debbie went alone on a trip with her grandparents she wrote back, 'I wish I had Kate in the car to fight with.' "[3]

Sharing

Warren, a surgeon, whose wife inherited a summer camp in Maine, invited his younger brother, Karl, to come up with his wife and children for their annual vacation. Karl and his family had a wonderful time and so did the cousins. The following winter during Christmas vacation, Karl invited his nephews to go down with them to Florida to visit Disneyworld.

This kind of sharing becomes almost a habit, a way of life in many families, but the ability to share willingly started long before this. It has had a long history in the life of the child.

When a toddler first discovers the word "Mine!" (next in importance to the word "No!"), it is a heady wine. Everything in sight becomes "mine"—including, "thine." Only after a long time and many tears does a child begin to understand the meaning and "value" of personal property, mine and thine. Later, children learn an even more difficult lesson, sharing and exchanging possessions with their sister and brother, not easy at first, but later backed up by experiences in nursery school or play groups. When children notice that their parents share love and objects with them and each other, they begin to feel that sharing must be safe because their loved grown-ups seem to enjoy it. Little by little, the high value put on sharing within the family is absorbed by the sisters and brothers along with their milk and Corn Flakes. And, if their rights are respected, the sisters and brothers come to respect the rights of others. Because they receive, they are able to give.

Paul, at four, having just discovered that his world could be safely shared with his younger sister, Amy, age one, was given two lollipops at the barber shop, and upon arriving home, handed one to her. Sisters, age seven and six, will share a box of cookies or a box of M&Ms that a friend of their mother gives them, counting out each cookie or candy equally.

About to leave school with his younger brother, eight-year-old Paul saw their much-loved grandmother appear unexpectedly. Instead of rushing over to grab her all for himself, he shouted, excitedly, "Hey, Ken, *Granny*'s here!" and they both rushed over to share hugs.

Sharing, then, can be of possessions and of loved persons, and is an important step in the development of closeness between brothers and sisters. Many younger children delight in helping to plan a birthday party for a younger or older one. They enjoy giving each other birthday presents, whether a drawing made by the youngest or a small gift bought by a slightly older one who saved up nickels and dimes for the occasion. Sisters and brothers may search widely for some item much desired by their sib. Sharing of one's "property" not only contributes to a sense of self-esteem and pride, but provides the added reward of being on the giving side, observing the expression of appreciation and joyous response of the recipient.

The Ultimate in Sharing

Perhaps the ultimate in sharing, or rather, sacrificing, is surrendering one's kidney to an ailing sister or brother. This act is truly a "gift of life." A healthy sister or brother—usually over eighteen—willingly and knowingly undergoes major surgery with the risk that any operation entails, emerging with postoperative pain and with no guarantee that the transplant will "take."

According to the *13th Report of the Human Renal Transplant Registry,* 2,461 siblings donated kidneys to an ailing sister or brother over a period of six years.[4] An inquiry to the Department of Health, Education and Welfare shows that figures are still rising.

Dr. Milton Viederman, clinical professor of psychiatry, Cornell University Medical Center in New York City, who works at the Rogosin Kidney Center there, points out that psychological responses of both donor and recipient vary. Much of the time things work out well, without any substantial difficulties. Siblings who had a good relationship previously continue as friends after the transplant. "But in nearly all relationships," Dr. Viederman continues, "some ambivalence is prevalent. The donor and recipient may both have anxieties about losing the kidney. Some postoperative depression on the part of the donor is not uncommon. He feels pain in addition to neglect. At this time, all the focus is on the plight of the recipient. The family hovers over the patient wondering whether the kidney will take or be rejected, how does the patient feel, and so on. Therefore, some resentment and sense of rivalry is bound to arise, in addition to guilt which is associated with the resentment."

However, when things work out well, the donor feels proud that he or she has done something for the family. Sometimes the kidney donation also becomes an act of restitution. A sister or brother who had felt denigrated, or who was the black sheep of the family, has a chance to be taken back again, respected, and valued.

Dr. Viederman has observed a common phenomenon. Often the recipient thinks: "This kidney doesn't really belong to me." "I must take care of my sister's kidney and not ski or take any risks with it." Sometimes the patient feels an obligation to accept some of the implicit demands or way of life of the sibling donor who may exploit this power. Should there be a discrepancy between their personalities, the recipient may feel a need to be *like* the donor.

Social pressures on an unwilling prospective sibling donor are enormous. The family may look upon a refusal as cowardice, a lack of love, and lack of family solidarity. Dr. Viederman extracted a few facts from a complicated case history in which sibling rivalry had been unusually intense among two sisters since early childhood. The sickly, older girl received so much attention from their mother that the younger one was pleased when *she* needed a hernia operation and could demand maternal attention. The younger girl married first, which made the older sister feel angry, jealous, and abandoned. The younger sister moved away partly because she didn't want to be the donor in a kidney transplant for her sick sister. She was virtually exiled from the family for a long time. The older sister, nevertheless, won a competitive triumph. She received her father's kidney![5]

The donation of a kidney to a needful sibling is not only a gift of life, but a sharing that indicates the capacity for love, courage, and sacrifice that few realize is possible between brothers and sisters.

Different Personalities, Different Lifestyles

No two sisters could be more dissimilar in looks, personalities, and careers than Rhoda and her sister, Brenda, in the TV series *Rhoda*. Rhoda has a successful career as a costume designer, is glamorous and attractive, has been married and divorced. Brenda, unmarried, works in a bank, is down-to-earth, has a great sense of humor and is both gutsy and "klutzy," stumbling over her two feet. Yet what comes through so strongly is the closeness between the sisters and their mutual need for one another.

"My older sister and I are on different wave lengths," says a sparkling, articulate woman. "I'm open and like to spill everything, but Helga, my older sister, keeps things in. I guess you'd call her an introvert. So it's hard for me to communicate with her and find out what she thinks and feels. But we get along in some odd, bumbling way."

We may say of sisters and brothers, "You'd never believe they came from the same family, dissimilar in looks and personalities, miles apart in their lifestyles and values. They seem to have little in common but the same set of parents."

Brothers and sisters change as their lives diverge. Circumstances alter them in a number of ways: a death in the family, divorce, illness, loss of money or job. Some go through great trials and come out with new strengths, greater compassion; others, having led relatively serene lives—from all outer appearances at least—turn bitter. Some sisters and brothers continue to develop in adulthood; others simply grow older but remain forever Peter Pan. Siblings may drift apart, not only geographically, but spiritually and psychologically. But whether a sister or brother becomes a policeman or politician, a homemaker or horticulturist, a screen star or salesperson, few sibs can write the other off. Our common roots, those inexplicable family ties, some mélange of sentimental memories, blood bonds, and a sense of "Yes, I am my brother's (sister's) keeper" holds siblings together. A sister says of her brother, "If we weren't siblings I'd never see David again because I don't care for the kind of person he has become. I still love him but I do not like him. Yet if he ever were in trouble, I'd be right there."

A short story, "Gifts," by Deena Linett in *Ms.* magazine,

tells of a sister who is about to let her brother know about their mother's death. She reflects, "In all the years since we've grown, college years, professional schools, marriages, we'd gone such separate ways, I suppose we didn't think it possible that we still had so much in common. Our childhoods were disparate, our adult lives even more so; yet there it was: we are brother and sister. The closeness of that tie remains unexplored since, countless generations ago, Antigone risked everything to bury her brother."[6]

A brother, born and raised in the deep South, moved up North and became a civil rights lawyer. When he returned South to join in some peace marches during the middle 1960s, his actions so angered his southern-born-and-bred sisters and brothers-in-law that they could barely speak to him for some time. However, underlying their enormous differences in values were bonds that couldn't be so easily destroyed. "Now," says this lawyer, "when I go back to Alabama to visit Kay and Mildred and their families, we just keep off the subject of politics, different ethnic and religious groups, and all goes well."

Events in life, or the turns we take in it, sometimes do leave us with little in common with a brother or sister. Yet, with it all, unless residues of rancor remain that have left ugly scars no one can repair, most of us manage to accept our uncommonness and still retain affection.

6
Siblings and Sex

Warren, a handsome and brilliant engineer, became vice-president of a large paper mill at the age of forty. He has had a rapid succession of affairs with women, yet remains a bachelor. He had grown up with two older "bossy" sisters, an overpowering mother, and a frightened father, who hid behind his newspaper during the arguments. His sisters constantly nagged him about his table manners, how he did his homework, etc., and, as he grew older, about his choice of friends and the way he dressed. He felt weak, inadequate, and angry, all the more so when, after he cried, sometimes out of sheer despair, his sisters taunted him with "real boys don't cry." When he began to seek out girls, as a teen-ager and adult, he overcompensated for his feelings of weakness by assuming a macho attitude, reveling in his conquests. Constantly searching for a woman to love, he would run away as soon as one became attached to him or made the slightest demands, in fear of being engulfed as he once had been by the women in his family.

The Beginning of the Battle between the Sexes

Sex jealousy between, and hostility toward, opposite-sex siblings has its origins in early childhood. As with same-sex sibs, an unequal balance of affection distributed to a sister or brother can result in sex favoritism. A mother may have been so disappointed by her husband that she attaches herself to her son, hoping he will compensate for her husband's lacks. Or a father with broken dreams his wife could not fill may invest them in his daughter. The jealousy between the opposite-sex siblings that arises under these circumstances can become unbreakable.

Warren grew not only to hate his sisters, but to fear all women, in part because his father failed to rescue his son from harassment and to protect his rights and dignity. He gave Warren no cues that it was good to be a male. Without such support, a boy with domineering sisters may withdraw from the battle, become intimidated and passive, or overly aggressive, exploiting women; his contempt an indication of his *fear*. Warren's sisters, however, also felt uncherished as girls. Their father kept out of their lives as much as he could, and their mother lavished all her love on Warren. Had these sisters received equal love from their mother, the chances are they would have taken great pride in their brother instead of trying to destroy him. The boy might then have acquired from them a capacity for sexual tenderness with women.

"Boys often pick up patterns of relating to women by observing how their father treats their mother and sisters," Dr. Walter Stewart comments. "If a father refers to them condescendingly and disrespectfully—'women can't drive cars,' 'that dumb blonde at the office,' or other such derogatory remarks—the father will thereby pass on to his son his low opinion of women." If, on the other hand, a father shows equal respect and admiration for the women in the family, a brother's feelings about his sisters will reflect this attitude. He might grow up to see women as persons of worth without feeling "inferior" or "superior" to them, thus reducing his own sex jealousy.[1]

A physics major at college claims that he never had these

problems with his three older sisters even though he was the youngest and a much wanted son. "Dad always included Laura, Carol, and Connie on excursions, but urged me to bring along a playmate. He was onto the possibilities of my being trampled on in a stampede, I later discovered. My sisters now tell me they were much too involved in their own sister imbroglios to give me that much thought as a rival."

A sister with several older brothers—bigger and louder —may feel a minority of one, yet her basic attitudes toward her brothers will also be determined significantly by other family relationships.

Patsy, now a fashion designer, had a happy relationship with her two older brothers and a younger brother. When she was very young, her mother and father—"liberated" long before their time—let Toby and Josh play with, cuddle, and nurture Pat's dolls, nor did they object to Pat's fascination with her brothers' pistols, cowboy hats, and boots. Their children had equal opportunity to try out all kinds of play, toys, feelings, interests, skills, and experiences. For several years, like many girls, Patsy ran around in jeans or a miniature track suit, refusing to wear dresses except on certain occasions. She trudged along contentedly with Toby and Josh in their adventuring. They, in turn, tolerated her, keeping a protective eye on their daring little sister, as she did later with the youngest. Until the boys were past seven and eight, an age when brothers tend to flock together with members of their own sex as sisters do with theirs (just watch any yard of prepubertal children at recess), they enjoyed her companionship. Pat grew up, as a consequence, with respect for herself as a person and as a woman and chose male partners worthy of her.

Patsy's capacity to enjoy her three brothers was influenced largely by her mother's own self-esteem as a person and by the quality of love she received. Through this extended life-line the daughter found she had an ally who enjoyed being a woman. Her father's love and pride in his daughter—and wife—reaffirmed his daughter's belief in herself as a female.

Dr. Stewart points out that, just as a brother reflects his father's attitudes toward women and sisters, a mother who calls her husband, present or absent, a "no good," or harasses him with, "Why can't you earn a decent salary?", or indicates in other ways that she considers him a nincompoop, will influence her daughter to see men through her mother's eyes. Her daughter, by extension, would be likely to see her brothers as members of the demeaned sex, and try her best to put them down or ignore them.[2]

It helps, of course, if there is another boy in a family of several sisters, particularly one near his own age, or, for a girl with brothers, another sister. The two of the same sex often build up strengthening alliances, modifying the dominating tendencies of the larger group.

Often, but not always, women and men who grow up in families of both sexes gain a deeper sensitivity to and understanding of the other sex. They learn, through shared activities and daily living, much about what girls and boys think are funny and sad, desirable and undesirable traits and behavior. All of this can contribute to a greater fulfillment for both sexes and broaden their perspective on life.

One other source of conflict and resentment between sisters and brothers, not to be overlooked, is envy of what the other sex is permitted or not permitted to do. Patsy's parents refused to put their daughter and sons into sex straitjackets, but many men now in their forties speak to me of having envied their sisters because of their freedom to express their feelings. They resented the fact that when they cried they were given scornful rebukes by parents who told them to "act like a man," or "don't be a sissy." When they fell down and hurt themselves as young children, they were less likely to be picked up and consoled.

" 'Keep a stiff upper lip' was the motto for the males in our family. We never dared express our anger or fears," says a former champion hockey player. Women now in middle age complain that they were told not to let their dresses get dirty or rumpled, not to roam too far from home, and not to cross their legs. A cosmetics sales manager says, "My mother would declare, 'How unladylike' in disgust about my 'tomboyish' behavior, when I *craved* the freedom I *believed* my brothers had, brothers who were told to act like 'little soldiers' and 'stand up straight.' "

Through the redefinition of these earlier views of what was considered "womanly" or "manly" behavior, today's younger brothers and sisters are reaping the benefits, while older ones come to see some of the "whys" of their sex antagonisms. As they are more infrequently cast into separate behavior molds, sisters and brothers may grow up with a greater understanding of, and respect for, each other's needs as men and women.

Sex Play between Brothers and Sisters

"I still blush mentally when I recall the time my brother showed me his thing and I showed him mine," a young grandmother confesses with an embarrassed giggle. Another woman showed no guilt whatsoever when she recalled that she and her brother laughed one day over their occasional childhood sex explorations. The two of them had felt daring at the time and remember how pleased they were to have "gotten away with it."

Childhood sex experimentation with siblings and/or other playmates has been part of almost everyone's experience. In their earliest, and normal, sexual curiosity, the younger children may have looked at or touched each other's genitals. With slightly older sisters and brothers, explorations may have become more sophisticated, thinly disguised as "playing doctor" games. The sex play of children, "If you show me yours I'll show you mine," has been popular since the days of Adam and Eve.

More often than not, parents are unaware that this research is going on, since brothers and sisters are apt to sense that such activities, if discovered, will not receive parental approval.

Perhaps the young grandmother who remembers with shame her normal childhood sex play with her brother had been made to feel guilty by some unnecessary and severe parental scoldings (by adults who, no doubt, had been severely scolded in their *own* childhood). A young law secretary says that for years he regarded sex as dirty and forbidden because when he was five his mother "shrieked" at him for examining his sister, age four. "I even avoided Janey for years because I felt I had done something evil to her." Because of the sense of guilt or shame one or both siblings may have attached to a shared sex "secret"—"I shouldn't have done it," "You used me," or "I used you"—some sisters and brothers have been known to deny this knowledge by avoiding each other even into adulthood.

Sometimes a child's mother makes a scene over experiments involving a disapproved-of neighbor's child (that nasty little girl!) because she believed it represented adult sexuality —which it didn't—or if more than two children were in the forbidden game, that it was group sex—which it wasn't. Childhood researches with the same- or opposite-sex sibling are likely to be accompanied by some sexual excitement, but the degree is usually commensurate with the child's age and development and a normal part of her or his growth, in any case.

Since children are so different in personalities and in inner and outer life experiences, not *all* sisters and brothers have engaged in these sex investigations or games. But what they did or did not do had little bearing on whether or not they were more or less sexually precocious, or more or less emotionally healthy or secure. Some simply had more curiosity and boldness than others. Some were afraid of their sibling; others had some inhibitions about coming to terms with the anatomical sex differences, or were inhibited because the incest barrier had already set in. Still others were used to seeing each other's bodies while bathing, toileting, and diapering, and had been told, reassuringly, about the genital sex differences and their functions, in a way that seemed to satisfy them.

Some words of Dr. Herman Roiphe, clinical professor of psychiatry at New York City's Mount Sinai School of Medicine, may relieve the minds of those adult brothers and sisters who still have some unconscious or even conscious guilt about childhood sex play. (These words may also have significance to parents of young children.)

Dr. Roiphe feels that parental intervention has always been unwise and uncalled for during "the kind of casual exploration that seems to come up now and then." If the parent has reason to believe, Dr. Roiphe says, "that the play seems excessive, highly charged, or unusually intense so the siblings can't seem to deal with it or get out of it, intervention is best carried out in terms of finding out what the children are really stuck on." Do they have mistaken notions about their bodies? Perhaps they need reassurance at that time about their anatomical sex differences, or further repeated explanations about them. Maybe other anxieties, Dr. Roiphe suggests, or pressures having less to do with sex than with other aspects of their lives are troubling them.

(Explaining anatomical sex differences to brothers and sisters goes a long way in helping them feel safer about their body intactness, thus also reducing some of the passing envies and the fears of siblings that perhaps they are missing some part of their body, or might lose it.)

Dr. Roiphe thinks a parent may need to step in gently but firmly "when an older sister or brother at a different level of sexual development involves a much younger sibling. What might be normal sexual excitement for an older child can be overstimulating for the younger one."[3]

A young child might have willingly submitted because she or he felt helpless, or may have enjoyed the attention and the activity, yet be confused and upset, not yet ready to understand what was happening.

A distraught mother says that her daughter, age five, reported that her thirteen-year-old stepbrother "tried to put his penis into me." It turned out that the boy had not entered the child but had rubbed himself against her naked body and ejaculated. In order to prevent any lasting shock to her daughter, the mother took her to a child psychologist, and, knowing that the boy had other problems since his father's remarriage, sent him to a child guidance clinic for help.

Sexual Awareness between Adolescent Brothers and Sisters

A woman recalls her distress when she was fourteen and her younger brother was thirteen. "For quite a while Tod kept criticizing me daily. One day he'd tell me I was too fat, or stupid. Then he'd say I was all pimply, which I was. '*Do* something about your hair, it's so stringy,' he'd say. And just yesterday we were sharing secrets and had been so close. Tod made me feel so unsure of myself because I saw myself through his eyes."

After having spent many years of childhood romping, wrestling, and in close daily contact with his younger or older sister, upon reaching, or after, puberty, a boy often finds himself drawing back and becoming uneasy about physical contact with her. J. D. Salinger's famous seventeen-year-old, Holden Caulfield, speaks with pride and tenderness about "Old Phoebe," his worldly-wise and pretty sister, seven years his junior. But he seems somewhat uncomfortable in one scene with his little confidante when he says, "She put her arms around my neck and all. She's very affectionate. I mean she's quite affectionate, for a child. Sometimes she's even *too* affectionate. I sort of gave her a kiss. . . ."[4]

Along with the marked physiological changes at puberty, including the tremendous surge in male sex hormones, a boy may be subjected to unwelcome and forbidden—to him—fantasies, some attached to his mother, and some, later, to his sister. Holden is dimly aware that his sister is female and draws back from physical contact with her.

To understand these feelings and fantasies, we have to touch briefly on the Oedipal period. A girl or boy between the ages of three to seven (or even earlier) develops erotic, sexualized love for the opposite-sex parent. This love is accompanied by jealousy of the same-sex parent—who is also loved—and the guilt and anxiety is so upsetting that after a while the child is almost forced to give up this "impossible dream" of possession, and represses it.

Such feelings then enter the unconscious mind. The child's love for the opposite-sex parent becomes affectionate and not sexual and she or he identifies with the parent of the same sex. Later, during the adolescent years, the Oedipal feelings with all their accompanying conflicts may come close to surfacing once more. Normally, if all goes well, these conflicts are permanently resolved and this erotic love for the cross-sex parent may progress outward from the family. The fantasies may transiently pass and settle onto the sibling then to an opposite-sex cousin, or aunt, or uncle. Ultimately, in this outward progression, the grown sister and brother learn to integrate their sexual desires and highly developed capacity to love with a partner outside of the family.

Usually, the mere thought that his sister is physically attractive is frightening to a teen-age boy and he feels guilty. His conflict may be further marked because he also has a strong fraternal affection for his sister. She is a "woman," however, a dangerous and tempting object, all the more disturbing because of her proximity. In the interests of psychological self-preservation, to assure himself that his controls won't break down, a brother, like Tod, may have to deny his sister's appeal by focusing on her faults instead. In this way he may be able to convince himself that she really isn't very attractive, and, therefore, safe.

"It made me furious when I was fourteen, and Vince, sixteen, would condescendingly refer to me as 'it' or 'the kid' —as if I were neuter gender," a young psychology student told me.

As Dr. Irene M. Josselyn, a psychiatrist, once said in *The Happy Child:*

> This depreciation of her keeps him free of any awareness that he might find her attractive since she is just as is the mother, a forbidden sexual object. This depreciation may be very threatening to his sister. If her brother sees nothing charming in her, she has little confidence that other boys will either . . . on the other hand, she is also reassured by his rejection because her brother is [also] for her a forbidden object.[5]

Adolescent brothers may feel overwhelmed by the strength of their newly discovered sex urges and capacities. Occasionally the sexual impulse has been so strong and the circumstances so tempting that there is some mutual fondling and touching between the brother and sister—her urges just as keen—but the guilt is so strong it usually stops right there. Sometimes a brother feels guilty for not having been able to subdue his fantasies if his sister herself—not *fully* conscious of her appeal—acts seductively. An adolescent sister may be well aware of her brother's sexuality and have somewhat the same conflicts. Her coquetry may not be altogether purposeful, but more as a part of her need to reassure herself of her physical attractiveness. Like many other sisters, she may breeze around in some filmy undergarment or bikini to tantalize her brother.

Several passages from *Young Lonigan* by James T. Farrell pinpoint these conflicts of both adolescent sister and brother.

> Frances came in. She wore a thin nightgown. He could almost see right through it. He tried to keep looking away, but he had to turn his head back to look at her. She stood before him, and didn't seem to know that he was looking at her. She seemed kind of queer; he thought maybe she was sick.

Somewhat later:

> Dirty thoughts rushed to his head like hot blood. He told himself he was a bastard because . . . she was his sister.

The two had been discussing friends and implied sexual behavior between them. Later, Fran, who is in bed without any sheets over her, asks Studs to get her some cold water:

> He handed the water to her. As she rose to drink, she bumped her small breast against him. . . .
> He left, thinking what a bastard he must be.
> He went to the bathroom.
> Kneeling down at his bedside, he tried to make a perfect act of contrition to wash his soul from sin.[6]

After an older adolescent boy has become attached to girls outside of the family, he feels freer to admire his sister overtly and to express affection. A middle-aged widow remembers an incident when she was fourteen that gave her the confidence she needed to face the terror of going to her first prom. "I went into my brother's room—he was seventeen then—before my date came to pick me up. He suddenly looked up and exclaimed, 'Gee, Sis, you look terrific! You sure are going to wow them. I wish I was your date!' My brother was very popular with girls, but before he began to go out with girls he hadn't seemed to notice me. His remark helped me to feel I was an acceptable female at an age where feeling accepted by the male sex had been so necessary in facing a crowd of strange boys."

Closely related to this reaction against regarding his sister as a sexual person are a brother's deepest feelings about her sexuality. In many parts of the world, if an unmarried sister has sexual relations, and her brothers hear of it, the result may be a vendetta to avenge both her and the family honor. The offender, if not killed outright, is severely beaten. The earliest brotherly vendetta reported in literature may be Absalom's slaying of his half-brother Amnon, who took Tamar, Absalom's full sister, against her will. In the United States, despite the sexual revolution and gradual disappearance of the double standard, many brothers still adhere to the protective code of "keep your hands off my sister." In one episode of a national television serial, *Eight Is Enough,* a high-school adolescent gets a black eye in a fight with a fellow student who has announced that since the boy's sister is going to appear nude in an amateur theatrical performance, he intends to take pictures of her to use as pinups.

Even though sexual mores may change, basic human feelings remain much the same. According to a number of family life experts, many boys, although unwilling to express their feelings overtly, would like to look up to their sisters as they do to their mothers. It is as if they are saying, "If my sister can be had by anybody, then I can't *count* on her. I want some stability and a sense of continuity in our family. We must maintain codes of behavior, otherwise we are lost." Although outwardly sophisticated and independent, many sisters also want to feel they can rely on their brothers' protection, steadiness, and sense of fair play.

Brother-Sister Incest

Whenever we read or hear or even think about incest—whether parent-child or brother-sister—we tend to recoil. Something deep within us makes us shy away from the subject. And for good reasons, too. A strong incest taboo has been built into us, handed down from generation to generation for thousands of years.

Legend, mythology, history, and literature have recorded endless evidence of incestuous brother-sister relationships and marriages. Such unions were sanctioned in some ancient civilizations, severely condemned in others. Gradually, however, any form of incest came to be seen not only as destructive to the family—ripping it apart in hatred, jealousy, and exploitation—but to society as well. The incest taboo was then written into the Mosaic laws and became, for the Judeo-Christian and other worlds a sin. This taboo is so strongly welded onto the structure of family life today that, by adolescence if not long before—regardless of fantasies connected with parents or siblings at certain phases of development—we all are aware that our sexual strivings are meant to find expression only in persons outside the family. The conflicts surrounding this taboo have been illustrated over and over again in literature.

Although the subject has never ceased to be of interest to writers throughout the ages and even today, not until the 1770s, the *Sturm und Drang* period leading into the romantic era of the early nineteenth century—that gloomy, despairing, daring, and tempestuous era—did a spate of literature on incestuous themes burst forth as it had in the days of ancient Greece and Rome.

In an exhaustive study of brother-sister incest in literature, history, mythology, and psychiatry, *The Children of Oedipus,* psychiatrist Dr. Luciano P. R. Santiago pursues this further. Goethe, Byron, and Chateaubriand, he points out, were among other writers and poets who had "uncanny bonds" to their sisters, and who wrote, not only in their works but in their letters of these guilt-ridden, impassioned sororal attachments.[7] Lord Byron's famous affair with, and love for, his half-sister, Augusta—with whom he had a child—seems to have been the only incestuous relationship among these writers that was acted upon. There is little proof that the others' attachments were anything more than fantasied, haunting passions for their sisters, causing tremendous guilt and a need for catharsis—an outlet for this guilt—through their writings.

Goethe's sister, Cornelia, was a year younger than he; both the only surviving children of six of a stern father and infantile mother. Goethe and Cornelia were constant companions in childhood, with few diversions and no supervision. Their attachment and need for one another continued into adulthood, but, eventually, Cornelia informed her brother of her decision to marry one of his friends. Although Goethe was involved at that time with another woman, Lotte, he writes, "I now first perceived that I was actually jealous of my sister; a sentiment I concealed from myself all the less, because since my return from Strasburg, our relations had become much more intimate."[8]

In many colorful passages in *The Children of Oedipus*, Dr. Santiago tells of Chateaubriand's great passion for his sister, Lucile, and of the deep conflicts within his family. Santiago describes a scene in Chateaubriand's novel, *René*, in which René speaks of Amelia, the heroine who like Lucile, was "the only person in the world I ever loved."[9]

Still in the Romantic era, but overlapping into the early Victorian age, other well-known men revealed through letters and histories romantic ties to their sisters, which, while deep and intense, were removed from sexual passion and strictly repressed. Perhaps these siblings never allowed themselves to know what they were really feeling. Words like "sacrifice" and "dedication" could well express their devotion. These famous sisters and brothers included Dorothy and William Wordsworth, Thomas Macaulay and two sisters, Margaret and Hannah, and Mary and Charles Lamb.

Macaulay had suffered a painful childhood relationship with a stern, righteous, and driving father. (Goethe's father, too, was stern; Chateaubriand's, impassive and uninvolved; Byron's father died when he was three.) Beginning in early adulthood, Macaulay turned his affection toward his two younger sisters, his juniors by ten and twelve years, who looked up to him and worshipped him romantically. Macaulay wanted to "outdo his own father" who had failed in maintaining "a bond of mutual trust and confidence with his children," as John Clive, author of *Macaulay: The Shaping of the Historian,* writes. But his affection for his sisters impeded his search for, or the desire to form, attachments to other women. Eventually both sisters married. Macaulay's reactions were hardly those of either a doting brother or real father. After each marriage he was plunged into deep depression. Quoting Sir George Otto Trevelyan, Clive writes that more than twenty years after Margaret's death, Macaulay found himself, "crying for her as if it were yesterday."[10]

Dorothy and William Wordsworth, nine months apart in age, were orphaned in childhood. Dorothy lived for the day when she could keep house for her brother. Her dreams finally realized, the two lived an idyllic existence in a cottage, totally absorbed in each other's company, working together and sharing an adoration of nature and literature. When William married, Dorothy, William, and Mary lived together in the same house and Dorothy continued her life's mission. In 1887 her biographer, Edmund Lee, wrote, "She simply dedicated to him her life and service, living in and for him. She read for him, saw for him and heard for him; found subjects for his reflection and was always at hand. Rejecting for herself all thoughts of love and marriage she gave to him and his her mature life."

Mary and Charles Lamb's intertwined lives were torn by his heavy drinking and by her recurrent mental illness and confinement in an asylum. In a letter to Dorothy Wordsworth he writes, "She would share life and death, heaven and hell with me. She lives but for me. . . . I know she has clung to me for better or worse."[11]

Clive refers to a number of similar sister-brother ties,

such as the Martineaus, the Disraelis, and the de Quinceys. Social values in those days, he points out, impeded early marriages for economic reasons, except for the relatively rich, and the morality of the era severely frowned upon premarital sexual experience. "Close attachment between sisters and brothers," he says, "therefore, were to be expected."[12] Opportunities for mingling with the opposite sex were also limited, and children sheltered from the world were often tutored at home.

One can see other problems in those days that led to overloaded fantasies attached to siblings of the opposite sex, or the sacrifice of a sister or brother to the life of the other. Either the children had had inadequate parenting or a poor balancing of family togetherness with the "otherness" of the outside world. Their emergence from the family seemed to have been blocked in some cases.

Incest Today

How prevalent is brother-sister incest? There is no accurate way of knowing. Statistics are hard to come by because most cases are not reported to the police, who keep these statistics. (Sometimes when a girl becomes pregnant and has a baby by her brother, she confesses, but not always.) Sometimes they come to the attention of hospitals, clinics, social agencies, and therapists. Usually brother-sister incest is kept secret because the siblings fear or do not want exposure. To increase the confusion, when consenting adults are involved, incest is a criminal offense, and when an older brother is the "perpetrator" or aggressor with a younger sister, incest is a felony labeled "child abuse."

Despite the lack of reliable statistics, there is no question that the lifting of the shroud of secrecy has caused an increase in reported cases of incest. Such cases, reported and unreported, of the acting out of incestuous sexual desires appear to be on the increase.

A study quoted by Dr. S. Kirson Weinberg, professor of sociology at Loyola College in Illinois, suggests that over a period reviewed, in New York City, there were about twice as many brother-sister cases of incest as father-daughter. But, as Weinberg indicates, the size and nature of the sample may not represent the country at large. In his own analysis of the subject, *Incest Behavior,* Dr. Weinberg studied 203 cases reported to the police in Illinois of which about 20 percent were brother and sister incest.

Were these families living in a Tobacco Road setting? Although the majority came from lower socioeconomic families, a few were from affluent families, and a number from middle-income families.

If some of the family members in cramped homes were predisposed to incest by personality factors and laxity in sexual restraints, the overcrowding, and especially lack of privacy, undoubtedly precipitated the deviant behavior. Many children had watched their parents have sexual intercourse, had slept together in the same beds, and had observed that adultery was tolerated.

Sometimes a sister had been initiated into sex relations by her brother when she was very young, but often the relationship continued even after the brother was married. Sometimes the sister was older and sexually aggressive and already sexually promiscuous outside of the home. Often the family became ingrown and isolated, bringing few friends into the home.

The family roles were usually unclear. Mothers did not act as mothers or fathers as fathers. Incest among siblings usually destroyed their relationship as sisters and brothers. Sometimes they became estranged from each other, or the girl looked upon her brother as if he were an eligible partner. In six cases the sister and brother had been separated or reared apart since infancy, and when they met again they fell in love. As Dr. Weinberg states, "Seemingly, they have missed the detumescent or de-eroticizing effects of a common socialization process as would occur from sustained association in a shared family life."

In some cases a brother may have been absent for many years due to war or other reasons, and when he returned, his sister, grown to physical maturity, became a sexually desirable object. "As a consequence," says Dr. Weinberg, "an incestuous liaison may ensue and then either terminate or become sustained depending upon the capacity of either of the partners to foster other relationships."

Because the parents had been "careless in supervising or indifferent to their children's sexual activities," the siblings had no incest taboos built into them, some having little guilt about their behavior. "Their sexual waywardness was further encouraged by community influences," Weinberg adds.[13]

It is easy to see why Dr. Santiago sums up the social purpose of the incest taboo in the following fashion:

It protects the young from being sexually exploited by older children and adults and it protects the latter from the sexual appeal of the young during their crucial stages of development so that they will be able to distinguish affection from sensuality. It prevents the chaos of confusing consanguinity as well as the ordeal of introverted families. Above all, it promotes wider interpersonal transactions and hopefully it will give rise ultimately to a community of man unbounded by clan, country, color or creed.[14]

It is obvious that incest is more likely to occur in severely disturbed families, or in those where both psychological and social pathology exists. Generally, through the socialization process, children grow up with a strongly built-in sense of the incest barrier.

BIRTH ORDER

7

Coming First, Then Paradise Lost

A father told me that experiences with his first child were felt more intensely by him and his wife than experiences with subsequent children though they loved them just as much. "Everything was unique, breathtaking, thrilling, frightening, nerve-racking, and certainly more worrisome." His son's first words, and first steps, were epoch-making events. "When Freddy graduated from school I wept. I was thrilled, too, at Amy and Gregg's graduation, but by then it was no longer something new."

Firstborns are usually talked to more, played with more, uninterrupted by the constant demands of other little ones. Every one of their questions seems to be brilliant, provocative, and worthy of careful, detailed reply. But when these same questions are asked by later children, many parents find their curious queries far less exciting, particularly when they must answer these questions while removing snowsuits, mopping up spilled milk, changing diapers, and other multiple tasks.

The Firstborn Mystique

The sun often rises and sets on firstborns. They are stimulated intellectually and enriched emotionally by exclusive and unshared contact with adults who care. They soon catch on to what is wanted of them, and, eager to secure highly prized affection, strive to please their parents. The parents' concentrated attention, however, brings tremendous pressure. Being firstborn is paradise, but it imposes high expectations. One man I know who was firstborn still broods because, as he told me, he was scolded as a child much more than his younger brother, who "got away with murder." Rosalyn Carter admits that with her eldest son, Jack, she and her husband were very strict. With the next son, Chip, "a little less." "And with Jeffrey—he was the baby—he got away with things the other two didn't. . . . And you know I thought if [Jack] did wrong, I was a failure as a parent."[1]

The mother and father become the firstborn's models, persons with whom to identify. Such special involvement with their parents often creates serious, studious, and highly motivated adults. Second and later children often copy and learn from each other even more than from their parents. Firstborn children learn language from adults; later children learn from children as well.

Historically, the birth of a first child has been universally heralded as an event for rejoicing and celebration. The arrival of a firstborn male child was cause for even greater festivity since the family bloodline and name would now be carried on. No greater sacrifice could be asked of a father than to surrender his firstborn son. God tested Abraham's love for Him by demanding as supreme sacrifice the death of Abraham's firstborn, Isaac, though He relented when He saw Abraham was willing.

Firstborn became crown prince, chief beneficiary of goods and estates, which, through the old laws of primogeniture, endowed the eldest with the lion's share of his parents' inheritance. Firstborns were often the best educated of all the children to prepare them to assume responsibility for managing the inheritance.

Such traditions from the past are not entirely dead. The

eldest male *or* female child still bears great responsibility; he, a juvenile among adults, must learn adult ways first. "The firstborn," wrote Alfred Adler, "is usually the one whom one accredits with enough power and common sense to be a helper or foreman of his parents."[2]

Psychologists now pay considerable attention to the study of birth order, to the ways in which rank in the family hierarchy affects personality, relationships with brothers and sisters, and with others in the outside world, including mates. Firstborns, studies suggest, tend to be dependable yet dependent on adult (or peer) approval, eager to agree with and placate others, anxious, conforming, and conservative—defenders of the status quo—and good at directing the work of others; they have respect for authority, sensitivity, a strong conscience, and an inclination to be studious, serious, introverted, egotistic, domineering ("bossy"), yet patient and protective.

A study by psychologist Dr. Richard L. Zweigenhaft of Guilford College showed that in a randomly selected group of members of Congress a majority were firstborns, but so were thirty-one out of a sample of thirty-five stripteasers. It was suggested that both politicians and striptease artists have marked needs for recognition, attention, and appreciation.[3] Certainly both expose themselves in one way or another to public view. Both invite applause.

A much higher number of firstborns attend top colleges and excel in the sciences, rank high among Rhodes scholars and in *Who's Who* listings. The controversy over nurture versus nature regarding intelligence and birth order has been going on for years. A 1979 report from the National Institute of Mental Health, "What Research Shows About Birth Order, Personality and I.Q.," indicates that in small families firstborn children tend to be "bright overachievers," especially males. According to this study, of 400,000 men in the Netherlands, aged nineteen, given I.Q. tests, firstborns received higher scores than laterborns. Another investigation in the United States, this report points out, involving some 800,000 men and women, drew similar results.[4]

A number of other researchers suggest it isn't greater native intelligence that results in such achievements but other factors. Parents usually spend more time with their firstborn child, who thereby receives more mental and emotional stimulation. Still other research points to the remaining traces of primogeniture. Families who had to scrounge to make ends meet may nevertheless set aside money to put the eldest child or first son through college. Little may be left for the next in line. Parental pressure on the eldest to achieve and fulfill parental dreams and goals also strongly motivates Firstborn. Psychologist Julius Segal of the N.I.M.H., while not striking out the importance of birth order, says, ". . . basic parental attitudes, values, and behaviors," subtly reflect on the child in the family environment and may have more of an effect on the child, "no matter what his or her place in the hierarchy of siblings."[5]

All of the findings regarding firstborns should, therefore, be taken with that proverbial grain of salt. Firstborns may not follow predictions. Dr. Robert W. White of Harvard observes that being born first doesn't mean that this inevitably or regularly "produces a certain pattern of personality. The findings only say that a certain pattern occurs just a little more often in firstborn children. . . ." Diverse experiences within the family also mold a human being's personality.[6]

Occasionally, however, some of these patterns do emerge in the lives of a firstborn. A commercial artist who, as a child, suffered terrible fears about taking tests at school, had recurrent dreams of surprise tests given when he was unprepared. His anxiety surfaced noticeably when he developed a habit of nailbiting. He was clearly and closely identified with parents who set up high hopes and goals for him, goals they did not place on the children to come. He, in turn, wanted their approval so much that he neglected his social life for work. His fellow students regarded him as aloof and stuckup. Actually, he was yearning to make human contact but could not.

In his late twenties, after seeking psychological help, this artist gave up his early desire to become a lawyer and concentrated on a newly discovered talent for drawing. He studied under less pressured circumstances and has taken great delight in succeeding at a vocation that held none of the anxiety that law held for him.

Dr. Lucille Forer, a Los Angeles psychologist, in her book *The Birth Order Factor,* suggests that "oldest children of both sexes tend to be seriously task-oriented, and will often ignore human relationships in favor of the work at hand. . . . They perform at a lower level when anxious. . . . When a firstborn is made comfortable, he will perform far better than when under pressure."[7]

Some of the resentments and misunderstandings known to brothers and sisters have their source in birth order. Each one may envy the other one's lot in being the eldest, middle, or youngest in line. Each may secretly resent the other for seeming more powerful or effective because of a preferred position.

Some children may also be affected by their parents' birth order in relation to theirs. Because some parents are able to identify more with the daughter or son who match the ordinal position they held in their own family, they treat them differently. Sometimes this means they "understand" that child's problems better or, to the contrary, project their own earlier problems derived from birth order onto the children who don't have such difficulties at all.

Needless to say, no one of us has a choice in being an eldest, middle, or youngest child any more than we can choose to be tall or short, or black or white. But brothers and sisters can be helped to *maximize* the natural advantages of their birth order and *minimize* its inherent difficulties.

The Next Child Comes, Intruder in Eden

"My mother tells me that when I was three, I filled my sand pail full of water and dumped it over my eight-month-old baby sister's head," a firstborn sister, an office manager, discloses. It took a few years of parental patience and understanding to help her get through her "hate phase," but the sisters eventually became lasting friends.

Attempts to push baby carriages down the hill, to spread pins on the carpet when a younger sister or brother is starting to crawl, to hug the baby while sneaking in a few nasty pinches, to try to push the baby off mother's lap—in these or similar ways firstborns may try to retain their treasured place in this primal contest for the love of their parents, especially the mother. Others try to get even with the usurper by suggesting, "Let's send Susie back to the hospital," "to Aunt Mary's," or, not to mince matters, "into the garbage pail!"

A onetime model who gave up her career to study medicine and become a psychiatrist, informs me that every time a younger model joined the agency, she had felt almost overcome by anxiety and jealousy. "I used to have dreams which went way back to my earliest childhood when each time a new baby arrived—and there were eight all told—I felt further and further pushed away from that long bread, or love line, to Mother."

The secure and favored position as Onlychild is lost when another baby appears to claim her or his share of the scene. We are bewildered to discover that this parental attention and love, particularly from our mother, is no longer exclusively ours. *And here is where sibling rivalry begins.* Freud participated in that experience himself:

Up to your nth year you regarded yourself as the sole and unlimited possessor of your mother; then came another baby and brought you grave disillusionment. Your mother left you for some time, and after her reappearance she was never again devoted to you exclusively. Your feelings toward your mother became ambivalent, your father gained new importance for you.[8]

Closely Spaced Births

There may be more trouble when the intruder arrives while Firstborn is still a baby.

A filing clerk admitted to me that she was cherished and adored by her parents for her first twenty-one months. Then a brother was born. Years later, in talking to her psychotherapist, she was able to recall that her child world "toppled down." She had felt utterly abandoned and "furious" at the shifting of her father's devotion from her to the new baby boy, and her mother's obvious joy and pride in having produced a male child. The sense of loss of paradise can be much worse if Firstborn is a girl and Secondborn a boy, or vice versa.

Loss of the prestige of being firstborn leads occasionally to lifelong hatred. Joan Fontaine arrived on the scene some fifteen months after her older sister, Olivia de Haviland, was born. When they both were very young, the two sisters were sent off to have I.Q. tests taken. Olivia had a fever on the testing day, and after the test was over she was informed that her younger sister's test results were much higher than hers. Fontaine now writes of herself, interestingly enough in the third person, in her autobiography No Bed of Roses:

Joan was undeniably her enemy. Besides the inexcusable intrusion into her life—that of Joan's birth—this latest display of arrogance was the last straw for the older sister. I regret that I remember not one act of kindness from her all through my childhood.[9]

A lifelong hostility was instilled in a boy who was nearly two years of age at his sister's birth. He never forgave her for being born. He had been the idol of his parents, grandparents, aunts and uncles, and now their attention shifted to her. Once, when he was five, he chased his sister around the house with a kitchen knife. In those days many parents believed children would outgrow their jealousy just as children outgrow their shoes. The boy never received help in reducing his inner anger and resentment and cherished his grudge years after he and his sister were grown up. On one of his rare visits to her, when both had adult children, he began to criticize her, angrily, for sanctioning the out-of-faith marriage of her son. In turn, she chided him for being so bigoted and intolerant. She couldn't put up with this kind of talk in her home, she said. His underlying hostility and jealousy turned what could otherwise have been a reasonably low-keyed difference of opinion into a wedge that separated them forever. Grabbing his coat and suitcase, he left in a fury and never spoke to her again for the remaining ten years of his life.

Does this mean that firstborns whose sister or brother is born after a longer space—say, when they were between three to five years old or older—have an easier time of it?

"Not necessarily," says Dr. Walter A. Stewart. "You can say that three or more years apart has certain advantages for the older child. He's had a chance to consolidate all his good experiences with his parents, and to grow. But you could also say that the trouble now is that he was used to all the attention for three or more years and he can't stand the change."[10] There are no simple answers in either case. Rivalry is bound to occur. The difference between enmity and friendship is what is done with that rivalry.

If a firstborn's emotional needs are still lovingly met by parents, if empathy rather than disgust is displayed over the child's difficulty in adjusting to the loss of primacy, and if the eldest comes to feel that there is enough love to go around, the intruder gradually becomes less of a menace and threat, perhaps a pesky nuisance, yet also a wanted and needed companion.

Some firstborns respond to their stress by giving up (temporarily) their hard-won struggles to grow up, returning once more to the gratifications of that lost paradise, regressing to infancy. They may ask for a bottle and nipple again, crawl instead of walk, suck thumbs avidly, wet and soil their pants, and more. These unhappy little firstborns may be unconsciously expressing their anger and disappointments: "What the baby is getting [attention] *I* want, so I'll be a baby again and get it." Temper tantrums, nightmares—which for children are usually a form of unconscious anger, and fear of the anger—increase. They may "quit" nursery school or day care so they can protect their vested interests at home. They especially want to keep an eye on Mommy so that their place with her won't be taken over by the baby while they are gone.

Jealous firstborns who are repeatedly told they are "wicked" and "naughty" may experience painful twinges of guilt for harboring, even if unconsciously, such "mean" thoughts. And guilt feelings, the most miserable of all, can lead to adult hatred of the secondborn who is the cause of their guilt. The eldest child, often more prone to guilt, may feel "wicked," aware that he or she is not living up to parental expectations. In all likelihood these feelings have contributed to anxiousness and a special need for approval and reassurance.

Some children, from the start, take things more or less in stride, displaying little resentment of the baby, sometimes paying little attention to the intruder. Many, slowly, begin to enjoy playing with their younger sister or brother, discovering the advantages of having a chum to guide and teach.

Those, however, who *always* seemed to "love" the baby, to please their parents, who were extra "good" or always eager and willing to help with the infant, may have been storing a time bomb underneath this placating attitude, ready to go off at some later month or year.

Dr. Sylvia Brody, a New York City clinical psychologist and psychoanalyst, describes the hidden jealousy and anger in a four-year-old firstborn, who instead of showing any signs of resentment toward the new baby and thereby risking the loss of her mother's love, played the part of a "perfect" sister "for several years." As she grew older, unexpressed hostility toward her younger sister and mother surfaced. She took over the maternal role and tried to mother and boss her mother as well as the younger child. Dr. Brody tells of another youngster, a boy of age three, who "ignored the entire episode of his dethronement by the baby who shared his room. Underlying fears, however, were uncovered when a year later he told of recurrent and terrifying dreams of mice, worms, and bugs which were filling up his room."[11]

These earlier happenings, long "forgotten," may not sour the relationship between the older and younger child if happier circumstances intervene, but some firstborns never forgive their sister or brother for having appeared on the scene at all. What seemed to the eldest as an outright rejection ("If I was good enough, how come you needed another child around?") may remain as a persistent pain. Some parents are convinced that firstborns will outgrow their attitudes, but such unawareness often further intensifies sibling imbroglios, and widens the chasm.

Firstborns may have every right to resent the second-born in the early years. Later, when and if a third or fourth sister or brother arrives—assuming that the firstborn's needs are not overlooked by the parents—they may be better able to cope than they were when the second child appeared. In addition, they now enjoy the special privileges allotted to an older child and denied to the others.

In some cases, as shown, firstborns may still carry—buried deep in their unconscious—some of the early resentment felt toward that intruder in paradise. No amount of growing up or passage of time ever completely eradicates the imprint of those "forgotten" memories.

Gap between First and Second

A woman remembers that she was five and in nursery school when her younger sister was born. She had, as she says, "a little world of my own there, and I thought I didn't mind Buddy's appearance until one day when my parents called him 'Baby.' I declared angrily, 'But *I'm* the baby!' "

Older children do not experience their dethronement as acutely as younger ones do, but they too remember the pain of their loss in the deepest reaches of the mind.

Other older sisters and brothers, although somewhat stunned and resentful at first, admit they were somewhat embarrassed by the baby's appearance because it was so obviously proof of their parents' sex lives—a fact that youngsters like to deny to themselves until past a certain age. Some report that their resentment was caused more by the change in their lives than by competitive feelings—which are usually there, nevertheless. And still others admit they had taken for granted that they were only children and had to make some inner adjustments that weren't all that easy.

"By that time I was moving away from home in a sense," says a college student who was twelve at the time of her sister's birth, "and I was happy that Mom and Dad took the hook off me and gave me more independence—something an only child often has to fight real hard for."

The Groundbreaker

Many an adult firstborn will recall that when she was young she had to fight hard for privileges, sometimes through constant nagging, needling, tantrums, tears, and door-slamming. By the time a younger sister reaches the age of her own youthful battles, these same privileges are handed to her on a silver platter.

"I couldn't go off to camp until I was ten," a high-school freshman declared, hotly, "and now Jack, who is barely eight is allowed to go!" "My younger sister (or brother) got away with everything," is a typical lament of firstborns.

No younger sister or brother really appreciates the fact that a firstborn sib was a trailblazer for the next in line and that the younger ones benefited thereby. The eldest may have paved the way for the younger ones although this was by no means their intention. Adolescents, in particular, are sometimes hard put because they are also the pioneers who had to take the plunge into new experiences without a close peer model after whom they could pattern themselves. Their fights for privileges may have been, at that time, permission to wear lipstick, to date, for extended curfews, to choose their own friends, for permission to take their first drink (openly), smoke their first cigarette (openly), use the family car, and to fit into whatever the lifestyle of their peers was at that time. Their parents, not yet having run smack into this teen-age phase, may not have understood that these demands were often—although not always—quite reasonable. To the utter dismay of one firstborn, after his hard-won victory, "There he went walking smoothly over the path I had paved with blood, sweat, and tears."

Many adult firstborns admit years later, that when they were separated from their younger brothers and sisters by going off to college, quite a few felt choked up as they said good-bye to "the pest," or "that kid," or "the chiseler," or even, "my gorgeous chic, younger sister who looked divine in a potato sack, while I, fat and with acne, looked a mess in the best of clothes." Their relationship, once a rivalry, may have become a meaningful companionship because of years of shared experiences. Accordingly, they may enjoy far more reunions with their sisters and brothers on vacation than with their parents (truly a bittersweet victory for parents who have brought their offspring to maturity). Sisters and brothers of college age may have found—unless a cold war between them has hopelessly dragged on—that the earlier frictions and jealousies have started to fade away. Although they may not always have approved of one another, their own sense of worth and dignity, their secure place in the family picture may have given them the strength to forge bonds to last a lifetime.

Responsibility and Protectiveness

A fifty-five-year-old lawyer told me he is still called in when there is a family fight, even though his younger sister and brother are now well into their late forties and early fifties. He is not called upon because of his expertise in arbitration, he says, but simply because he is the oldest.

Hortense, a lab technician, told me that her five younger sisters and brothers, her juniors by a few years, feel she is "the veteran of the world. I've been treated as nurse, mother, oracle, and psychiatrist. Most of the times I enjoy being the 'adviser' but at other times I'd like to abdicate."

Firstborns usually enjoy being in the driver's seat and more often than not they have to fight hard to maintain their position of authority when younger ones seek to snatch their power away. But, like Hortense, other firstborns would have been willing to take a back seat and not always have to look after the younger sisters and brothers because their own dependency needs were often overlooked.

The capacity to be helpful with and responsible for others is, in part, the result of having first been on the receiving end of the same in early childhood. Eldest brothers and sisters absorb these attitudes from the adults around them, gradually finding satisfaction in helping their younger sisters or brothers as discovering that they, as older ones, can solve problems. These discoveries also strengthen their feelings of adequacy as persons. Without too much prodding from their elders, firstborns begin to take pride in their responsibility to younger, more helpless sisters and brothers. Such "doing" for someone else adds to the feeling, Dr. Sylvia Brody points out, that "we're a family and are always going to help each other."[12] A perfect example is the older child who sacrifices his or her future and goes to work to send younger sibs through school and college, especially if one or both parents have died.

When his mother was ill for a short time, one older brother, age seven, was thrilled with the idea that he could get out milk and butter from the refrigerator, make toast, and pour cereal into bowls for his five-year-old brother and three-year-old sister. After his mother recovered, he voluntarily asked to continue his "job."

Responsibility as a Burden

A number of adult firstborns, however, also complain about the burdens of responsibility they had, always told to "keep an eye on Susie and Freddie," which sometimes kept them from playing with friends. Older brothers and sisters often speak of the time upon reaching puberty, or even before that, "when I wished that little nuisance wouldn't always have to tag along." Many remember the days when they were dating and would bribe little sister or brother to go to the movies.

Sometimes grave responsibilities were thrust upon firstborns before they were mature enough to handle them. Heavy responsibilities in younger days may increase First-born's tendency to become serious and overly conscientious. Too much responsibility is apt to increase the eldest sibling's resentment of the sisters and brothers for whom they are responsible. And if they fail at their job or mission—if anything happens to the younger ones in their charge—they suffer severe guilt and remorse. The worst thing any older brother or sister can be told is, "You should have had more sense. You should have known better—you are the *eldest!*" Or, even, "Act your age!"

"I still shudder at an experience which was very traumatic for me and potentially dangerous for my younger brother that happened when I was seven years old," a noted photographer told me. "For years after this event took place, I bucked as much responsibility as I possibly could. I always felt I would fail again. One day, Mother told me to take complete charge of Micky, age three, while she went on some shopping errands. Soon my pals beckoned to me to join them in their play. I was miserable, but suddenly I got a bright idea. I would tie a clothesline around Micky, hitch it up to a tree, giving him toys and ample room in which to play. As it would happen, Micky managed to slip out of the rope and ran quite a distance down the street where there was traffic before I noticed his disappearance. When Mother returned—after I'd found Micky, unscathed—she scolded and punished me severely. I learned very little from the punishment or incident, because, I guess, I was much too young to really understand the implication of my responsibility. But I felt that I had done something *terrible,* both to Micky *and* Mother."

One little girl, who was turned into a nursemaid and baby sitter by her mother, is now a divorcée and in analysis. "By the time I was nine," she says, "I was feeding the five younger children, bathing them, putting away their toys, scolding, rocking, and soothing them. I had no time at all for friends, and later they interfered with my dating to some degree. Yet in some strange way, I enjoyed my grown-up position." In her analysis, however, she discovered that she had felt overburdened, and more important, that she had been deprived of sufficient maternal love and care herself. Without being aware of it at the time, she set out to mother the babies just as she would have liked to be mothered and babied. Taking on a mother's role helped her to forget that she had ever felt deprived. "For years after, when I was grown up, I continued to feel I had to mother everyone and 'rescue' them. Underneath, it seems, I hated being saddled this way, for I complained to my analyst, 'My friends all come to me with their troubles,' or, 'I always have to get them out of a mess.'" In an extension of the same role, she took on her friends' problems; it could help her to forget her *own* need for support. "What I really wanted down deep was to be given oceans and oceans of love, lots of babying and attention myself—all and more of what I had never received, and become the recipient of all the love I had given out to others."

Many other eldest sisters and brothers have been known to put their younger sister or brother through college, as mentioned earlier, either by working and giving up their own chances for a higher education, or by scrimping during and after college to help the younger one have the same opportunity. Many of these oldest sisters and brothers have felt it their duty and responsibility to make such sacrifices, and may also have made these gestures out of love and kindness.

In large families, and to some degree in small ones, brothers and sisters often learn much about mutual dependency and responsibility. Turn-of-the-century novels show the firstborn was not required to take on so much responsibility. The care of younger children was divided up among all of the elder children, and someone was always helping another down the line. Frequently, parents, grandparents, aunts, uncles, and other members of the extended family were around to back up the sibs. The younger ones shared assigned chores.

Guardian

Protectiveness often comes quite naturally to the eldest. While their mother and father went off for a few days of much needed rest, nine-year-old Kevin and his younger sister Anne, age five, stayed with their grandmother in her house outside of London. The grandmother described the children as "alternately fiendish and angelic, fighting like mad at one moment and then showing tenderness to each other in the next." One evening, several days after their arrival, Anne called down to her grandmother, sadly, "I don't like this holiday." Kevin quickly followed his grandmother upstairs, leaned over his sister's cot and said, lovingly, "Are you homesick, my pet? It's horrid, isn't it? Now you just go and have a little cry and you'll feel ever so much better after." A few tears rolled down Anne's face. In less than two minutes she cheerfully joined the other two in the kitchen downstairs where they all made applesauce from the apples picked from the garden.

Older children may try to protect the others from punishment and join forces against the parent. One of the rewards that can come to older children who are in charge of younger ones is the satisfaction of educating them about the world and its ways. This point is beautifully illustrated in an early section of Alex Haley's *Roots*. Eight-year-old Kunta somewhat reluctantly takes his younger brother along with him as he goes off to play, but soon finds enjoyment in teaching the boy about nature, explaining how bees make honey by sucking the sweet flowers. Haley writes, "And Lamin began to ask Kunta a lot of questions, most of which he would patiently answer. There was something nice about Lamin's feeling that Kunta knew everything. It made Kunta feel older than his eight rains. In spite of himself, he began to regard his little brother as something more than a pest."

When he sees his younger brother has been knocked down by a fellow goatherd, Kunta rushes over, shoves the boy away and exclaims, angrily, "That's my brother!" After that incident, Lamin started to copy whatever his brother did. "Though he pretended not to like it, Kunta couldn't help but feeling just a little proud."[13]

Younger children may react to protectiveness with gratitude or to superior power with resentment. For example, a younger sister says with affection, "I am fifty-four now, and my sister, five years older, still clutches my hand tightly as we cross streets—just as she did when I was a child." But a disgruntled man resents his brother's lording it over him. "I always had to fetch and carry for Alan, my oldest brother, when I was younger, and he irritates me even today because he hasn't stopped thinking that 'brother knows best.' "

A younger sister says of her older brother Gene, who is five years older than she, "He has always been like a father to me because Dad died when I was seven, and he's always there when I need him. But even when I don't, he's all too ready to hand out advice to me."

"Ned is such a worrier and perfectionist about himself and the rest of us in the family," says the nextborn of three brothers, now twenty-eight. "But he always was so shy and awkward with the girls that *I* gave *him* some know-how on how to approach them, and, boy, I felt proud!"

Mopsey Strange Kennedy, a family therapist, who is the youngest in her family, writes in *Newsweek:*

> In the scant years and months before we were born, these firsties were out there learning serviceable facts and lapidary truths, acquiring a stance of certainty, an air of leadership. An oldest of any age has this over a youngest of any age. My own firstborn daughter, while technically twenty-four years my junior, has her mitts on some wisdom that makes her seem magically my senior.[14]

Yet, as Firstborn sees it, life is not always such a bowl of cherries. The oldest child often lives in that twilight world between parents and children, mediating between the generations as deputy parent, pioneer, and champion of younger sibs. As Firstborn reaches adulthood—parents having long shown their eldest that the younger never displaced him or her—some of Firstborn's "bossy" tendencies may be converted into high aspirations and constructive challenges in the wider world. If the child is not exploited as a surrogate parent, Firstborn's attitudes toward the younger siblings may become loving and protecting.

8

Secondborn, Coming After

Some of us may remember that our mothers or fathers always took the side of a sister or brother who had been the oldest, youngest, or middle child because—as we can understand now—*they* had felt at a disadvantage in that particular birth order position. In reality, sometimes it is another child who is in need of encouragement or protection.

"My parents have no compunctions about telling a story on themselves, the outcome of which made all the difference in my relationship, to the good, with my sister," Angela, a schoolteacher, said to me with humor. It seems that when Angela was about three years old, she had frequent temper tantrums—always when her older sister, Laurie, was returning home from nursery school. Her parents couldn't find any reason for this strange and upsetting behavior. Wanting to help her because she was so unhappy, they consulted a child psychologist. It developed that her mother, and to a mild degree her father, had been very disconcerted at having a second girl, although Angela was enchanting.

"Mother had been very envious of her own younger sister who was blessed with an irresistible charm from the day she was born. The psychologist got her to see and under-

104

stand that unconsciously she was identifying with Laurie, feeling guilty that she was placing her firstborn into the same situation that had caused her own suffering." Angela explained that her mother felt she should have presented her firstborn girl with a younger brother, not a younger sister. As if to make amends to Laurie, she displayed obvious partiality by making a big to-do about her, ignoring Angela when Laurie came home from school.

"And, of course, Mother told me years later that it was also her unconscious resentment of me, her younger daughter—the 'intruder'—like her own sister, that was felt so acutely by me. All I remember is that things seemed ever so different at home after a while and Mother was as loving and dear to me as she was to Laurie."

Competition for "that inestimable prize of life"—as the child sees it—to be the parents' most loved; competition for possessions, competition to be heard and accounted for is sharper when there are two children (or even three) of the same sex in the family and where the age difference is not too great.

Characteristics of the Secondborn

A variety of studies on birth order describe secondborns as cheerful, outgoing, pragmatic, expressive, innovative, stubborn, nonconforming, independent, rebellious, more involved with peers than with parents, capable of being deceitful, regarding themselves as considerate of others, diplomatic, and good tellers of jokes.

Secondborns have been found in large numbers among revolutionaries of various sorts. In *The Washingtonian,* Susan Seliger writes that Frank Sulloway, a visiting member of the Institute for Advanced Study in Princeton, New Jersey, has carried out research on more than one thousand scientists who had taken stands on some major revolutions in scientific thinking within the last four centuries. Some of these controversies were over the theories of Copernicus, Newton, Darwin, and Einstein. "In each case," Seliger writes, "Sulloway says he has been able to document that a majority who favored the revolutionary ideas were laterborn scientists, while over eighty percent of those who steadfastly resisted the new notions were firstborns."[1]

Once again, caution and discretion are in order. Not all secondborns fall into these categories. Inborn personalities, life experiences may make their imprint and a person emerges with different features. Yet there are good reasons a second child may display some of these traits.

Secondborn children generally have an easier time of it than do their predecessors. Parents, so earnest and concerned with that all-important firstborn, are now more experienced and relaxed. They have learned from Firstborn what a baby's cry may mean. They have discovered that thumbsucking and toilet-training are not all that important. And, easing the pressure on themselves, they are now more comfortable and better prepared to enjoy Secondborn. Many parents are inclined to be more indulgent, to have greater tolerance of the secondborn's lapses and shortcomings, to expect and demand less. In part, this comes from their increased confidence as mother and father, in part, from the fact that their hopes and expectations are still focused more intensely on Firstborn.

In any event, Secondborn is the beneficiary. The softer, less rigorous atmosphere encourages him or her to be more easygoing.

Secondborns may start life more serenely, but gradually, as they come into conflict with the people around them, a fervent desire emerges to "become as old as the first, by outdoing him in skills, in games, in strength, in possessions," as sociologists W. Allison Davis and Robert J. Havighurst write in *Father of the Man.*[2]

Fairy tales, history, and legend tell of younger brothers who try to take over, or succeed in defeating the elder. In fairy tales about two brothers: "The Story of the Youth Who Went Forth to Learn What Fear Is," and "The Soldier and the King," the youngest wins out over the older through kindness, valor, generosity, or wit.[3] Jacob, the younger (twin), cunningly seized his brother Esau's birthright (primogeniture) in exchange for that "mess of pottage" when Esau was ravenous for food. And he tricked his father, Isaac, into giving him the elder brother's blessing. Miserable Prince John tried to wrest the throne away from his brother Richard while Lionheart was off crusading. Shakespeare offers us Hamlet's Uncle Claudius, who not only poisoned his elder brother but usurped his crown and wife as well.

Secondborns learn at the outset to adapt. As soon as they are aware of their surroundings, they learn that Firstborn got there ahead of them. They quickly see that the love and attention of their parents must be shared (not always willingly), unlike Firstborn who sees an unwelcome invader threatening his or her unique and privileged position.

Catching Up

In replying to a question on how he felt about being the younger of two brothers, a Los Angeles candidate for a degree in hospital administration told me, "For years I never could catch up to Bert, my senior by three years. I felt as if I was climbing a steep mountain with my arms always reaching up to get to the next rock which my brother had already passed. But I gradually learned a trick or two on how to get others to take notice of me. Today I feel fairly adequate about myself even though somewhere within me lurks some of those old self-doubts about my competency—even though Bert hasn't made a smashing success of his life or of his work either."

From the time the eyes of the secondborn follow the

movements of their busy all-round-the-clock ready-made companion, the younger children continuously strive to catch up to what was—for the moment—their hero or heroine. Efforts to communicate with Firstborn early in the game are strong, unless squelched by the older one's efforts to become the younger one's ventriloquist, interpreting for Secondborn. Soon, however, as secondborns become a little older and the "me too" theme—all children's cry for "equal rights"—becomes prominent, the younger ones begin to catch on to the fact that they are at a keen disadvantage.

An observant father, a writer who worked at home for several hours of the day while his wife had an outside job, made this comment about his two boys who were eighteen months apart, four years old and two-and-a-half. "My younger boy seemed to be compelled by an inordinate drive to achieve and perform tasks which he saw his older brother accomplish with ease—at least that's the way it appeared to him. I worried that he might be stretching his physical, psychological, and mental muscles beyond his capacity." And his wife added, "It was as if he were saying, 'Anything you can do I can do better.'"

As many brothers and sisters may recall, their older sib often invited them graciously to play a game comprehensible to the older but not the younger child. Then the older brother or sister—say an eight- or nine-year-old—often became exasperated when the younger one just couldn't understand the rules of the game, or, as it sometimes was, *her* or *his* rules. Both children then became angry and frustrated. After these trials, secondborns were convinced that their older brother or sister had more strength, intelligence, and power. Thus the power struggles began.

In his book *The Uses of Enchantment,* on the value and meaning of fairy tales in enriching the child's inner life and in helping children to cope with the psychological problems of growing up, Dr. Bruno Bettleheim talks about a young child devastated by sibling rivalry:

A child can see things only with subjective eyes, and comparing himself on this basis to his siblings, he has no confidence that he, on his own, will someday be able to fare as well as they. If he could believe more in himself, he would not feel destroyed by his siblings no matter what they might do to him. . . .

. . . if the child could only believe that it is the infirmities of age which account for his lowly position, he could not have to suffer so wretchedly from sibling rivalry, because he could trust the future to right matters.[4]

Unfortunately the future doesn't *always* "right matters" and even at the age of seventy or more, sometimes an older brother or sister can make a younger sib feel like the assistant to the assistant to the manager.

Hand-Me-Downs

Hand-me-downs are the life story of secondborns (third-borns, etc.). What younger sister or brother didn't inherit secondhand clothes, equipment, books and toys, a battered doll, a dented truck, faded pajamas? (And the oldest sib may not have been overjoyed to see the younger take over his or her possessions, however beat or outgrown.) "I always accepted hand-me-downs from Dennis without complaining, but when Mom gave me Doris's parka I blew my top!" a bank vice-president still remembers with some bitterness. Although parents may need to stretch clothing and toys over a whole family for economy's sake, younger sisters and brothers who are loved know that their mother's and father's love and affection are not secondhand. Then material possessions don't tend to interfere with their basic sense of self—which counts the most.

A fond grandmother loves to tell the story of how her seven-year-old second grandson replied to her question about his T-shirt. "Haven't I seen that shirt somewhere before?" "Sure you have, Granny," he said with pride, "it was Ted's. It's not new for *him* any more but it's new for *me.*"

One college senior remembers that "Once, Aunt May, mother's younger sister, came to my rescue by buying me a brand-new scarf to wear with Jenny's old snowsuit, and it sure made the outfit appear quite different. She often helped me this way. And when I could get something brand new, Mom would let me have the fun of picking it out, even when I was only four."

Another younger sister, now in her late thirties, whose overly cluttered home and bursting closets betray much about her need to be loved—surrounding and covering herself by things in order to compensate—tells how she had felt unloved by her mother and father. "They couldn't be bothered with us; they were always on the go. Each season Mother would spend a few minutes going over Ellie, my older sister's clothes, deciding what would fit me and what wouldn't, caring little about whether or not I liked the dress or coat. But as soon as I could earn money I bought everything in sight and reveled in my own new clothes and possessions."

Compensations

While younger children may resent all the advantages and privileges accorded their older sister or brother, such as staying up later at night, being allowed to cross streets alone, or having a larger allowance—"It's not *fair!*", "She gets to do *anything!*"—they may not realize that they profit from their older sibs' pioneering.

There are compensations. When the eldest gradually moves farther away from the family hearth—barring the jealousy when a sister or brother begins to date and seems to be leaving out the younger sibs—secondborns can see that they are moving up to a higher rung of the family ladder with a senior's prerogative if a new baby has arrived.

A young, glamorous grandmother talks about the ways in which she was able to profit from her older sister's bitter experiences. "Wilma, at thirteen, just struggled and fought with Mom to gain the tiniest bits of independence for herself. Every minor issue became a major confrontation. I vowed that I would avoid this turbulence at all costs when I got to be thirteen. Three years later when I reached that age, I just went 'underground,' and appeared docile as a lamb, acting compliantly—at least on the surface. But I quietly went my own way, keeping most of my actions as well as my feelings, private."

In *Newsweek,* Mopsey Kennedy again renders her cryptic protests: "Also, many parents, having taught Firstie, find themselves all taught out and leave their other children to their own education."[5]

Having found it difficult to be in the lead position at home with a same-sex older sister or brother, younger children often gravitate to same-age playmates outside of the home and find satisfactions there on a more equal basis. Here they can get opportunities to be leader and "boss." Secondborns are often "joiners," more outgoing and sociable than elder sibs (who *sometimes* find it more difficult to make friends because they have been more used to adult company).

Secondborns often try out one identity after another until they come up with one that fits and suits their purpose. One chubby youngster, the second male child, noticed he could attract attention by playing the clown. He became the court jester to the appreciative amusement of his mother and father. Successful at his early efforts to amuse, this boy gradually developed a remarkable wit and sense of humor, talents that became great assets in his adult life. Secondborns can become masters at getting their way, and "getting around people."

Some psychologists have observed that in order to have

others take notice, secondborns (much like girls who are not as pretty as their sisters) often develop charm and personality that their competitor may lack. Secondborns, who are apt to be friendly, often derive some of their greatest satisfactions from friendships and social activities.

9

Middle Child, the Human Sandwich

A seventy-two-year-old middle sister of three fell and broke her wrist. A few days later a niece went to visit her. As they were talking the aunt burst into tears and wailed, like a little child, *"Your* mother was sent through college when I was fifteen. Every remaining penny, which could have put *me* through college, was spent on Amy's voice lessons, and for the preparation of her career. I was given *no* lessons of any kind and yet, knowing I could do so much with my hands—paint, sew, and make beautiful things—I became a pioneer in occupational therapy, all on my own. If my wrist doesn't knit properly what will become of me?"

The special predicament of the middle child has been vastly neglected in research. Here is that child, wedged in like the contents of a sandwich between two slices of bread where she or he can't be seen. More than that, for this sister or brother, it is clearly a case of "two's company but three's a crowd." No longer the baby, the child has neither the position of prestige held by the eldest, nor that of appealing helplessness enjoyed by an infant. The middler has a less defined role in relation to parents as well as to the family. Somehow these middle children have to struggle even harder to strengthen their shaky sense of identity. (First-borns are sufficiently removed in age from the newest arrival that often a third baby poses no real threat to them, many taking real delight in amusing or occasionally helping to nurture the infant.)

Middle children may feel particularly left out if they are of the same sex as the older child but followed by a sibling of the opposite gender, who, of course, brings extra excitement.

On the other hand, in families of three or more, psychologist Dr. Lucille Forer observes, "Self-esteem is generally high if the second is the only one of his sex in the family."[1] This does not mean that the child will be necessarily favored, but it does mean that the second at least has a certain distinction and compensation that goes along with his or her ordinal position. A copywriter in an advertising agency told me, "I felt I was living in the best of all possible worlds when I was a young girl. Grant, my senior by two years, was always *my* champion, and I could be little Tim's, my younger brother, guardian. They both considered me special."

Middle children need help in coping with what seems to them an unfair, even *untenable* situation. Just as with the very young firstborns, when the new baby arrives, they use the most primitive tools to help them master their crisis. Sometimes they make great demands for attention because they need it. In time, with encouragement, they, too, may learn to adjust.

To assure herself of top billing one middle-born young lady of four insisted on having full attention paid to her every word as she told of her daily doings. Like Scheherazade, she spun a new tale every day. "And," her older sister comments somewhat acidly, "she hasn't stopped talking since."

Spurred on by the need to be heard, those in the middle may learn to use their potential to the utmost. Later in life, having learned to be flexible, to adapt and negotiate with both younger as well as older sisters and brothers *and* parents, middle youngsters may become career diplomats in their relations with others.

Middle children are often spared some of the demands placed upon the oldest children and the restrictions placed on the youngest. Among parents who tend toward acute anxiety about their offspring, more often than not the middle children escape some of the intensity of anxious concern. Some middle sibs may become lost in the shuffle, especially in larger families, their human need to feel special and distinguished unsatisfied.

Alliances may be formed between the eldest and youngest sisters and brothers, with the eldest taking on a quasi-parental role with the youngest, leaving the middle child stranded until, or if, another child comes along. Then numbers two and four themselves become a team. At least in one women's college, sister classes are the odd-numbered and the even-numbered classes (all freshmen have junior "sisters"). One psychiatrist suggests that even numbers in sequence among siblings may make alliances easier, and that the competitive situation may be exacerbated by the odd-number family, the two older thus lining up together and the two younger ones lining up together, leaving middler out again. The psychiatrist observes that where mutual dependency or interdependency exists, and a distinct feeling of "we're all in this together," flourishes, the middle child becomes a part of a close and loving unit.

Groucho Marx, the famous middle of five brothers, had a warm relationship with his brother one up the line, Harpo, and with the next down the line, Zeppo. Of Harpo, he said with humor in his autobiography, *Groucho and Me,* "He inherited all my mother's good qualities—kindness, understanding, and friendliness. I inherited what was left."[2]

Once when Groucho was ill Zeppo filled in for him, and Groucho "discovered to his glee that his baby brother could match him point for point in delivery. . . ." To give his brother a chance, he kept out of the show for two weeks.[3]

The personality of the middle sib, of course, affects each one's experience. The balance of power in a three-member or even larger family depends on how the individual middleborn responds. Some are naturally quiet, serious, and unassuming; others sparkling, social, and independent, and far more interested than others in relationships outside of the family. Others are even more assertive. Some have no trouble whatsoever in maintaining their status and give it little thought. Some seem to shrink into the woodwork; some exert themselves to be noticed.

Middle Child—Same or Opposite Sex

The competition for the limelight may be even stronger if the middle child is one of a three-child family of all males or all females. "I was pushed around by my older brother and then I was supposed to take it easy with my younger brother. I felt all boxed in as a child," declares a man who has done nicely in both professional life and as a father.

In the words of a middle sister, who is a retired beauty shop owner and manager, "I used to feel out in left field because Rowena, my older sister, was especially close to Antonia, my younger sister—almost like a second mother. However, when they got into fights, who did they come to but me to settle their disputes. I refused to take sides but helped them make up again. Soon I began to be known as the family peacemaker and it's continued that way ever since."

One middle girl of fourteen was told by her friends, "You let your sisters walk all over you." But she didn't see it this way at all. The girl felt quite secure about herself; she was even-tempered but would quietly stand her ground with her sisters if need be.

In another threesome, the middle boy, a rather strong-willed fifteen-year-old, who had been used to wheeling and dealing in his relationships, played the game of two against one, and would side with the older against the younger, or with the younger against the older, so that automatically he became the powerful one. However, as the youngest boy himself grew in strength, the alliances shifted. More often than not, the middle boy found the oldest and youngest ganging up on *him.*

It is not at all unusual—if parents aren't right on top of this situation—for a middle child of the same sex, particularly a boy, to withdraw from competition, feeling that in being quiet and unassuming, in placating everyone and keeping out of the way, he'll be more loved.

But in many other families of same-sex siblings, each child is made to feel that its place is special. Parents of three daughters refer with equal pride to "our eldest daughter," "our middle daughter," "our youngest daughter." Each designation sounds, in their voice, cherished and unique.

Some middle children claim that if the two older children are of the same sex and the youngest is of the opposite sex, the two older ones will become closer companions than either is to the other-sex child. Yet, as they grow up, the youngest and eldest may find that they have more interests in common or that they are kindred spirits, regardless of sex or interests.

Larger Families and Middle Children

In larger families, jealousies, often intense in small families, are frequently reduced. Sisters and brothers form so many different, ever-changing cliques, factions, and pairs that each youngster nearly always has some champion to turn to. It is not unusual for the middle child or children to become a henchman to the older same-sex sibling. And, often, since the older sibs are so far removed in age, the younger child looks up to the middle sister or brother.

Indeed, Groucho Marx, right in the middle of two older and two younger brothers, emerged as the leader of all his brothers. His son, Arthur, writes about the famous Marx Brothers team:

> Father had taken it on to himself to shoulder the responsibility of running the team. *He* was the one who showed up at the theater early to rehearse the orchestra and the actors. *He* was the one who dreamed up new material. . . . And *he* was the one who made the financial arrangements and argued with the management when things weren't to their liking.[4]

Sibling feuding does exist in large families, as it does in smaller families, Bossard and Boll point out in *The Large Family System*. "Large family living makes for pressure upon its members and pressure makes for competition."[5] Nevertheless, they say, children in large families quickly get together to defend each other in quarrels that are soon over. Grudges don't last long.

10

The Youngest, Favorite of Folklore

In their book *The Sibling,* psychologists Brian Sutton-Smith and B. G. Rosenberg report a survey they conducted of 112 of Grimm's fairy tales. "In 20 percent of the stories, there were three children; the first and second children won only 8 percent of the time, but the third child won 92 percent of the time!"[1] (All of these children were of the same sex.) "Winning," of course, meant triumphing over the meanness, selfishness, or even the treachery of older sisters or brothers.

In Grimm's "The Queen Bee," Simpleton, the youngest of three brothers, is sent out by his father, the king, to find his two profligate older brothers. He is successful, and on their way home, Simpleton proves to be resourceful as well as kind, though his brothers think him foolish. He protects some animals a brother wishes to destroy. In the end, the grateful animals come to his rescue when he has to master ever more difficult tasks. The queen of the beehive, whom he has saved, helps him choose from among three identical sleeping princesses the one who is youngest and most captivating (the favored youngest again). Naturally, Simpleton marries her and inherits her kingdom.

"The Griffin," also in Grimm, tells of three sons who are sent to bring apples to a princess. On the way each meets a man who asks them what they carry. The two older ones, thinking to protect their gifts of apples, lie, and the man's magic transforms the apples into the worthless things the brothers said they had. The youngest son, who has been derided as Stupid Hans, tells the truth and he alone arrives with the apples and wins the princess.[2]

Why has the youngest been so favored in folklore?

Fairy tales and myths, transmitted from generation to generation, represent the collective experiences, hopes, fears, and psychological conflicts of mankind in barely disguised form. Some have suggested that younger children, having long been low man on the totem pole, finally wove their discontents into the fabric of these tales, thus providing themselves in fantasy with a fulfillment of their deepest wishes. Others have suggested quite the contrary, and maintain that among large families the last child may have held a most-favored position and that this is the way things really were. Another interpretation is offered by Dr. Bruno Bettelheim, who discusses the appeal to children of those tales in which the youngest of three is considered as a simpleton at first, but, in the end, proves himself to be superior. He explains that a little child often sees himself as foolish. Though highly intelligent, he may feel inadequate in comparison to others above him who seem so knowledgeable and capable. These feelings about himself "are projected not so much onto the world at large as onto his parents and older siblings."[3]

Two Extremes: Dependence and Independence

Perhaps all these interpretations make sense. In many instances, the youngests' ordinal position does offer rewards. They may be stimulated and helped by their parents and sibs to gain independence, often at an earlier age than their older sisters and brothers did. The youngest, then, may become self-starting, adaptable, and creative children and adults. But the opposite might happen. If older sisters and brothers have overpowered the youngest, the youngest may continue to follow in their shade. They may be compelled to remain "the baby" of the family even into adulthood, enjoying yet resenting their dependence. It may seem an impossible task to shake off this dependence and establish themselves as individuals in their own right. One young woman, an ecologist with several older brothers, puts it this way, "It took me years and years to establish my credibility as a *person,* because my older brothers continued to see me as 'little kid sister.' Like all minorities I had to work ever so much harder than the others for validation so that they—in this case my brothers and parents—would sit up and take me seriously."

Many children struggle between these two polar positions, wavering between wanting to be independent and free, yet wanting to be indulged and dependent—a common conflict of all humans. Lucky are those who reach the ultimate compromise and discover the joys of being both interdependent and independent.

The outcome for the youngest is largely determined by the way their parents experienced their own childhoods. Did they ache, as children, to catch up to the older ones? Were they envious of the "spoiled, rotten" baby in their midst? Did they place importance on their children's autonomy because theirs was crushed, or fostered? Or did they prefer to keep their children dependent upon them because it made them feel so needed?

Undoubtedly, Youngest may often have felt tempted to remain the baby of the family if the child saw or felt he or she would always be coddled and pampered, able to make demands on parents and get away with it.

Perhaps this is part of what happened to Maria, the youngest girl in a family in which a brother was the oldest, followed by two sisters. Her attempts to grow up were smothered by these older girls, who competed with each other in raising their "little doll." Their father died when Maria was six and her sisters were eleven and twelve. The mother, who

carried on her husband's restaurant business, was too exhausted by the time she returned at night to take charge, or
even to take notice of what was really going on. She was
grateful that the two senior girls were willing to take over for
her. (Their brother, seventeen, was at college on a scholarship.) As the years went by, the parental sisters picked on
Maria for every little shortcoming, advised her on what to
wear, what friends to choose and how to behave with them,
what courses to take at school, and much else. When she was
eighteen they were still running her life—even deciding
what vocation they felt best suited her. Her own feelings of
inadequacy prevented her from even thinking of breaking
away. At nurses' training school, a supervisor fortunately
recognized her difficulties and suggested psychotherapy.
Maria began to take life into her own hands, make her own
decisions and mistakes, and free herself from emotional ser-
vitude and bondage to her sisters. (It must be added that a
good deal of guilt and sense of obligation toward her older
sisters had prevented her from taking any action earlier.
They had often commented on how much they "sacrificed"
to raise her, without noting that they had also gained much
satisfaction from their "job.")

No doubt the youngest learns much from the experiences of older brothers and sisters—if learning is not *im-
posed*. To the youngest, the counsel of older sibs often rings
louder than any edicts pronounced by on-high and "old-fash-
ioned" parents. After all, younger brothers and sisters have
plenty of opportunity to watch their elder siblings' lives in
action. These young men and women of wisdom—in the
youngests' eyes—have tested the world outside; the youngest
can profit from some of their goofs as well as from their
victories.

Striving to catch up to older sisters and brothers works
out well unless the younger ones try to overreach themselves
and tackle projects, activities, and problems that are beyond

them, their exertions ending in frustration, discouragement, and further feelings of insignificance.

A former airline stewardess, now the director of public relations for a large airline, tells this story about herself as told to her by her parents. Her father, a former ski champion, had said, "You had made it, kid, by the time you were three or so." Her mother agreed. "You were a joyous, lively two-and-a-half-year-old, when you followed Alex, then five, and Scott, seven, just about everywhere. Since you wanted to choose your clothes because Scott and Alex did, we let you; since you wanted to dress yourself as they did, we let you do this to a degree. Even though almost everything went on backward, we felt it best not to interfere and let you develop a sense of autonomy.

"A year later," her father went on, "you could nearly match your brothers in endurance on long walks and climbs —you were a real 'trouper.' But then, suddenly you'd reach up to be carried. We weren't deceived by your wish to be 'big' but recognized your needs to be held and cuddled and babied at times—typical of children your age who take giant steps ahead and then retreat like a turtle into its shell."

"At supper you managed to get in your two cents' worth," her mother took up the story. "You had plenty of opportunity to play with other children your own age at nursery school and get a chance to relax and compete less. Your brothers, as you soon found out, took great pride in you and even helped you 'entertain' your first boyfriend at the age of three! You never were in danger of being submerged or overwhelmed."

The Youngest of Same-Sex Siblings: Finding One's Place

It is more difficult to find your place in the world when older sisters and brothers are of the same sex. Some time ago, a French psychologist, analyst, and educator, Dr. Charles

Baudouin, in a book called *The Mind of The Child: A Psychoanalytic Study,* said that rivalry appeared as one of the most "violent conflicts" in Victor Hugo's unconscious. Hugo was the youngest of three brothers, a puny child who "nurtured a secret ambition to be considered the equal of his older brothers, to outstrip them and 'take their place.' "

When such desires arise in early childhood they usually find expression in a wish for the rival's death. Such a wish is in reality less cruel than appears on the surface, for a little child does not know what death really is, and, not infrequently, uses the word as a synonym for "absence." All through the life works of our great poet the numerous ramifications of this unconscious theme may be followed in all their details. But he happened to be a genius and was able to sublimate in a truly beautiful manner his infantile complex of rivalry.[4]

A politician, now in his fifties, describes this incident: "My two older brothers were great athletes, but I seemed to have two left feet and was just miserable that I couldn't get on any team at all. But Dad had a brilliant idea. He told me I was so great at pleading, arguing, protesting, why didn't I go out for debating at school? I followed his advice and became so good at this 'sport' that I was elected president of the debating team in my sophomore year at high school."

In the words of a woman who told me of her childhood fears of developing her talents because of *three* elder sisters, "Since Vi went to art school, Phyllis to dancing school, and Lily to dramatic school, I took it for granted that I didn't have any of these talents." Later she herself won dancing contests as well as major parts in school dramatics—and without lessons.

In an article in *Ms.* magazine, "The Extraordinary Simon Sisters," by Jane Shapiro, the youngest of three unusually attractive and successful young women, relates her own struggle. Carly Simon, a well-known pop-rock singer, was third in line of children of one sex. "If you have a strong ego, as I did, what do you do?" Her eldest sister was "always sophisticated, always poised and theatrical." Her second sister was "shy and angelic and sweet and soft and adorable. I remember thinking, literally, that I had to make a conscious decision about it; to decide who I had to be. The ingenue had been filled. The sophisticate had been filled. So I chose my role. . . . The comedian hadn't been filled yet."

Carly Simon speaks of a situation not uncommon with younger brothers and sisters; sometimes a type of guilty fear of succeeding over an older sibling sets in. Her analyst got her away from living with her eldest sister, "the big sister, the all-powerful one, where I was stuck in the same family role I'd been in my whole life, where it was better to be defeated than successful. I moved out . . . got a band together . . . got a recording contract. Started to fly! It was the most acceleratedly productive period of my life."[5]

Who has it best? Who has it worst? Carly's mother understood her daughter's problems and encouraged her as best she could. One of the keys to the outcome of relationships between eldest, middle, and youngest sibs has always been parental recognition of the special pressures that might weigh on brothers or sisters in their particular place in the family. As each growing child's belief in her or his unique capacities is fostered, the fear that he or she might just become a mere shadow of an older brother or sister, or suffer a compensating and compelling need to overshadow that sibling is overcome by the happier and more lasting experiences of friendliness, mutual pride, succor, and love.

11
Twins,
the Unique Siblings

Irma, an identical twin who is now twenty-seven, remembers clearly her great anxiety when she first went off on a trip without Sandra. Although she wanted to find her separate self, she didn't want to lose what she still thought of as "my other half." "I always depended on Sandra for everything. We knew each other's every thought. I never trusted myself away from her and was terrified of going away to camp alone without her, but my parents believed it would do both of us a lot of good. They were right. Although it was a wrench getting away from 'us,' it was a joy to discover 'me.'"

Just as with sisters and brothers in any ordinal position in the family—and the one born first is considered the eldest —twins suffer jealousies and rivalries, hidden or overt—only more so. They tend to be closer to each other than do other sibs. But from the start each twin has shared a special need, and that is to become a "me," and not just a "we." In order to enjoy fully the special pleasures twins can share, each has needed to carve out an individual self from this sometimes cloying togetherness.

The mystery of twins has inspired legends, myths, and literature. It is said that the biblical twins Jacob and Esau began to fight in their mother's womb. Legend has it that twins Romulus and Remus were nursed by a she-wolf. Famous among mythological twins are the heroes Castor and Pollux, whose devotion to each other Jupiter rewarded by turning them into heavenly stars: Gemini, the Twins. Shakespeare, said to have fathered twins, used the twin theme in two of his comedies. In *Twelfth Night,* Viola believes her adored twin brother, Sebastian, has perished at sea. Donning man's attire, she so resembles him that when Sebastian reappears there is general confusion as to who is which. *A Comedy of Errors* has mix-ups over two sets of identical twins, each with identical names, distinguished only by their cities: Antipholus of Ephesus and Antipholus of Syracuse, with their twin attendants, Dromio of Ephesus and Dromio of Syracuse.

Many parents and grandparents of today's adult generation were spellbound by Lucy Fitch Perkins' twins series concerning girl-boy pairs from the world over—*The Dutch Twins* and *The Japanese Twins* were only two of about twenty-six similar titles—and the much loved *Bobbsey Twins* series by Laura Lee Hope, first published in 1904 and still going strong.

Why are twins so appealing to young and old, and why do they so strongly capture our imaginations? One explanation offered is that some of us have long-forgotten childhood yearnings for a twin. Who can't remember when as a child we weren't good and mad at, or disappointed in our mother or father and felt misunderstood and alone? It is at those moments of disappointment and anger, says Dorothy Burlingham, of the Hampstead Child Therapy Clinic in London, in her classic book *Twins: A Study of Three Pairs of Identical Twins,* that many school-age children cherish a common daydream of a wish for an "understanding" companion, a twin. This partner, the child imagines, will always be available to him and "give him all the attention, love and company he desires and who will provide an escape from loneliness and solitude."[1] Some children pretend to talk to this imaginary twin who, they hope, may bring them added strength and power.

Some Facts about Twins

It is generally accepted that there are two types of twins.

1. Identical twins result from a single egg fertilized by the same sperm splitting off into two individual eggs. They have the same blood type, the same fingerprints, hair texture, and color of hair and eyes. Most identical twins look alike. In about 25 percent, moles or dimples or other markings may appear on opposite sides of their faces, and hair-whorls go in opposite directions, a physical phenomenon called "mirror-imaging." Sometimes this also appears in a left-handed twin whose writing may go backward.

Their identical genetic inheritance plays an important part in their development, although studies of identical twins raised apart have shown that they often display totally different interests, skills, and even temperaments, stimulated by the way their parents respond to them, by the particular background in which they are raised, and by their individual life experiences. Because each set of identical twins is different from other sets—as is each child within that twinship—it has been found that some but far from all of such twins reared apart or together *may* be prone to similar physical illnesses or psychological disturbances, sometimes appearing around the same time. They all become gray or bald at identical periods in their lives. "My brother and I developed cavities in our upper molars at about the same time," writes a twin approaching thirty.

2. Fraternal twins evolve from two separate eggs fertilized at about the same time by two separate sperm cells. Although born as twins, they inherit an assortment of different genes, just as do any other siblings. Fraternal twins can be of the same sex and bear some resemblance to one another, or there may not be any resemblance at all. Or they can be opposite-sex twins, resembling each other to some degree, or not at all.

The Benefits and Problems of "We-ness"

As many twins will admit, having or being a twin is not always a golden dream. Twins share very special problems, as well as benefits—more so than other sisters and brothers.

Only by going back to the earliest days of childhood can twins, friends or relatives of twins, or others interested in them understand how their joys and sorrows may begin.

The twins' special alliance, the "we-ness," has its strong points, particularly in providing mutual support. At times they function as a self-contained unit. "It was hard to buck my little seven-year-olds when they planted their feet squarely before us, declaring, 'We have made up our minds that we're old enough to cross streets alone!'" a mother of twins notes.

Having grown up fairly independently, with distinct personalities, while also sharing many similar tastes and experiences, one set of identical twins enjoyed performing as a duet on occasion. Both took high honors at elementary and high school, were star athletes, bringing victory after victory to their school as successful opponents of other school teams. Wherever they went they enjoyed their triumphs as a team, and were considered VIPs whose presence brightened up parties and school festivities. They also engaged in competition between themselves, alternately winning or losing, but this rivalry was offset by their common goals, activities, and loyalties. When they became teen-agers, their personalities were so distinct that they never sought the same girls nor did the same girls seek them.

A number of twins have teamed up together to make quite a splash in the same careers. The late Drs. Guttmacher —Alan, an obstetrician and gynecologist, past president of the Planned Parenthood Federation of America, and his twin, Manfred, well-known Washington, D.C., psychiatrist— are among a number of famous twins in medicine. Scientists

Auguste and Jean Piccard worked together and separately as explorers of the stratosphere and ocean depths, enjoying numerous successes. In the creative arts, one pair of outstanding twins is British playwright Anthony Shaffer, author of *Sleuth* and *Frenzy,* and Peter Shaffer, who wrote *Equus* and *Royal Hunt of the Sun.*

The special closeness starts almost at birth. Babies soon become aware that they are not alone. They hear each other's sounds and coos in the crib or carriage, and often are soothed by them. At first they may not know where one of them begins and the other ends. One baby twin was found sucking the thumb of the other. If separated or if one of them dies in the early months, a twin may fret and thrash around restlessly searching for his or her partner and have difficulty in sleeping.

An adult identical twin says he recently entered a restaurant and nearly crashed into a mirror as he walked toward it believing his brother was coming over to greet him from another room. Even though it may appear so this is not what is meant by a psychological "mirror-imaging!" Twin babies and toddlers often tend to see each other as a reflection of themselves and often mimic the actions and moods of the other. A mother of fourteen-month-old boy twins asked one of them, "Where is your mouth?" and he proceeded to touch the mouth of his twin. Marjorie Leonard, a child therapist from Stamford, Connecticut, gives another illustration of this process in identical girls, age five, who were trying on dresses, "Lacking a mirror, one of them said to the other, 'Stand over there so I can see how I look.' "[2]

In his famous novel *The Bridge of San Luis Rey,* Thornton Wilder, also a twin, tells about Manuel and Estéban, identical twins who developed a secret language early in life. "This language," Wilder writes, "was the symbol of their profound identity with each other."[3]

Between the ages of about two and three or earlier,

when twins spend a lot of time together without much stimulation from adults, they sometimes communicate with each other in a language all their own, understood clearly by themselves, but by no one else.

Normally, unlike the twins in Wilder's novel, by school age or earlier—provided adults close to them spend considerable time talking with each of them—they catch up with other children in speech, relinquishing their private language. Occasionally, if the language doesn't disappear, a speech therapist is called in.

Overwhelmed and exhausted mothers of baby and toddler twins have reported, "It's so wonderful that they can keep each other company and entertain each other. Then we can get some much needed rest." And rest is needed. But as results from psychoanalytic case histories of some adult twins have shown, this ability to entertain each other, and being left on their own constantly, or for too long a period, can cause them to form overly strong attachments to one another which interferes with, and weakens the bonds they should have formed with their mother and father. Instead of taking cues from their parents as to behavior, some of these twins become each other's mentors in early childhood, thereby delaying the strengthening of each individual ego and personality or the development of a firm sense of right and wrong.

Twins are much less afraid of being alone in the world, away from that twin to whom they are so closely bound, when they have received early *individual* loving play, cuddling, and holding, from their mother, father, or some warm and caring substitute mothering person. These experiences help twins separate sufficiently from one another to identify with their elders and look to *them* for early approval and disapproval. It helps each child to be relished, loved, and known as an entity.

"From the time I can remember, we were dressed like

two peas in pod, until we were in eighth grade," Loretta, now a graduate student in philosophy, recalls somewhat sadly. She told me that "Cassie and I—whose personalities clashed tremendously for a while during our teen years when we began to see how different our natures were—didn't stand a chance for individual freedom."

Outsiders seem to get a kick out of lumping twins together as a unit, encouraging them to see themselves as Xeroxes of each other. It is especially aggravating for some twins when outsiders declare, "Aren't they cunning." "How can you tell them apart?" Yet other twins have declared they thrived on togetherness—again, until they reached puberty, when one girl twin brought home a boy and he fell for the other one. Some twins object strongly to being referred to as "the Jones twins," or even as "the twins." Or if they have been given whimsical rhyming names, Ronny and Donny, Sharon and Aaron, or Winny and Pinny—names which make them shudder on becoming adults.

"How can you establish your dignity, how can you become a separate entity when you're always on parade, considered part of a sideshow or as one of the Seven Wonders of the World?" a young naval lieutenant miles away from his brother but close in spirit asks.

Some twins insist on matching their clothes and fooling people as to which is which. "But," a grown twin admits, "the trick did become tiresome after we were a little older, when people were always calling us by the wrong name." An older sister of twins says, "Judy and Patsy desperately wanted to wear identical clothes, but the rest of us encouraged them to at least select different colors, or to add some accessory that might help each feel distinguished from the other." Other family members recommend that some individual possessions belong to each twin, and arrange for separate visits to relatives, overnight stays with friends—short and not forced separations—to help each child realize that his or her life pattern need not always follow the same one as the twin's.

Differences and Comparisons

Whether identical or fraternal, twins often have different temperaments. One may be more outgoing, the other, quieter; one may be the leader or be more aggressive, the other, the follower. With some twins there may be a seesawing effect. One will dominate and lead for a while and then the roles may alternate. Not infrequently this shifting comes to an end and the personalities become set, more or less, into one pattern.

The firstborn—even if by a few minutes—often assumes leadership. However the leader, the more assertive twin, is frequently but not always the one who is heavier and stronger at birth. We do not know Jacob and Esau's respective birth weights, but we are told that Jacob, the second twin, was born hanging onto Esau's heel. He soon took over —not fairly—and later became the leader of the twelve tribes of Israel.

Secondborns may accept their senior's leadership but resent the "older" twin's advantage, just as any younger child does. They may strive hard to achieve prominence. Other secondborn twins may unconsciously feel apologetic, feeling they are intruders who deprived their older twin of his prerogative—the undivided love and attention from the mother. The firstborn of one pair was always referred to as "Jack" and the secondborn as "the twin," which confirmed "the twin's" feelings that he shouldn't have been born at all.

Twins dislike being compared. Two nonidentical twins, one in training to become a medical technician, the other an office manager, give their own versions: "People expect you to have the same attitudes, tastes, values, and thoughts," Carol, the trainee, remarks. "They'll ask, 'Why don't you look like your sister?' as if it was my fault that I don't, and, of course, you must gather that Joany is prettier than I. 'Are you the brainy one?' 'Has Joany or you got the most boyfriends?' You can't get away from being compared and from feeling that you have to be better at something than your twin—even if you don't care about being outstanding in some way." Carol admitted to me that since she and Joan now live in separate apartments and lead their own lives, they get along much better than they did as children.

In the words of Joan, the office manager, "You know, I was always more independent than Carol, but people would insist, 'You're the more dominating twin, that's for sure.' But I wasn't. Sometimes Carol took the initiative and sometimes I did. We just faced and handled our problems in different ways. But can you imagine, although Carol was a much better student than I, *she* used to cry when *I* was scolded for not getting higher marks?"*

Another problem more accentuated for twins than for other sisters and brothers is that of school performance. "By the time we were in sixth grade," a brilliant newspaper columnist admitted, "it seemed obvious that my twin sister was going to be an A student, and I, a B-minus one. The teacher suggested putting us both into separate sections of our class. From that time on I gradually lost my feeling that I wasn't as bright or capable as Gloria, and my marks shot up. Even more important, I not only felt I was being judged on my own merits, but I found new friends. It was a relief to discover I could stand on my own two feet." (This newspaper columnist, a nonidentical twin, is now the mother of twin boys and knows what she is about.)

But other twins are less fortunate. In one set of noniden-

---

*Although referring to toddlers, Dorothy Burlingham points out that when one twin was scolded the other would act guilty too, which is a normal outcome of the identification "of two beings of the same age and in the same stage of development living in such close proximity."[4]

tical twins, the older, more aggressive of the two, tyrannized over the younger. He was at the top of his class, his brother at the bottom, although their I.Q.'s were virtually identical. When the time came to go to college, the younger refused to go and stayed at home, no doubt afraid of a new failure. It took him two years to regain his confidence and start out on his own.

The performance of identical twins whose I.Q. is remarkably the same—give or take five points—may not always match their innate abilities, often because one of the twins does not feel as able or as competent as the other and gives up. Still others, twins of both types, often find their twin a sort of security blanket. Feeling dependent, they resent any attempts others may make to separate them. Usually at puberty the partners become more mature and want to strike out on their own.

Rivalry and Competition

From the moment of birth twins have to share possessions, including the most treasured of all, their mother, whom they do not share willingly or graciously, particularly at feeding times.

Very young twins—watching each other's every move—become aware quite early that one may be quicker than the other. A twin may become distressed as she or he notices the other one crawling, standing, or mastering some feat sooner. The seemingly disadvantaged twin may take longer in "getting there" at first, but sometimes later proves to be more agile. Nevertheless, the slower twin profits through help and encouragement.

As they grow older some twins love to see the other one excel, especially if it is in areas in which they are not competing. Competition often has a different quality for identical twins. One high school senior commented seriously, 'It's no fun losing to Jerry, but it's no fun winning over him, either."

Observations of identical twins suggest that they often will dodge competition to avert the antagonisms that might arise between them. They may feel, unconsciously, that by letting out their (normal) desire to win out over the other, they'd be opening a Pandora's box full of hidden, maybe uncontrollable feelings of aggression and hostility, along with inevitable feelings of guilt. Due to their mutual identification, such a twin might feel unconsciously that "hitting my twin would be like hitting myself." Therefore, they may seek ways of denying their rivalry. Sometimes they escape these feelings by sticking together as much as possible, sharing and dividing their food and possessions equally, *always* trying to even things up. They may also divide up their parents; one may latch on to mother and the other on to father.

Sports writer Herbert Warren Wind gives a striking example of how inhibited competitiveness can work, as he describes the behavior of the famous Renshaw twins, tennis champions of the 1880s. Both young Renshaws were handsome and greatly admired by their fans. Willie, the elder identical twin—born fifteen minutes earlier—was outgoing, and liked to appear in amateur theatricals; Ernest, the younger, was not as self-confident, and stammered. Wind writes in *The New Yorker*, "His [Ernest's] forte was the accurate placement, and he had a finer touch than Willie. In addition, he was faster on his feet. . . . However, Ernest declined to play Willie in the Challenge Round in Dublin. It was typical of Ernest to defer to his slightly older brother in nearly all matters, and he particularly disliked opposing him in tournaments."

When Ernest was finally persuaded to meet Willie, on two separate occasions in the Challenge Round, he lost to his twin in both of them. In one of these contests, many observers departed with a hunch that Ernest had probably thrown those last two sets. At the other Challenge, "Some people, knowing how intransigent Ernest was about the importance of being Willie, were not a hundred percent certain that he had gone all out in the final set."[5]

Reluctant as they may be to face their rivalry, twins would do well to understand that some competing between them is inevitable and won't hurt their relationship unless the rivalry becomes constant and bitter. After all, in their hot disputes, or even fist fights, twins are usually more fairly matched than are brothers of different ages. It is expected that they will "fight it out" occasionally through games and sports and arguments, as long as they play fair.

Same Wave Lengths of Identical Twins

Some identical twins feel as if they are on the same wave lengths because they often have the same thoughts and feelings at the same time. Adult twins living apart have reported how they wrote letters to each other at corresponding hours and dates, and how, unknowingly, made plans that coincided with the other's plans. A Colorado lawyer, whose twin brother (also a lawyer) lives in Virginia, informed me of the day when he selected an unusual book for his twin's birthday only to receive the very same book from him for the very same occasion.

Wilder's Manuel and Estéban were none too happy in their twinship because their resemblance caused them to be the target of comments and jokes they did not find amusing. They tried not to appear in the streets at the same time or they went along different streets. "And yet," Wilder writes, "side by side with this there existed a need for one another so terrible that it produced miracles as naturally as the charged air of a sultry day produces lightning. The brothers were scarcely aware of it themselves, but telepathy was a common occurrence in their lives, and when one returned home the other was always aware of it [even] when his brother was still several streets away."[6]

A number of authorities on twins feel there is no mum-

bo-jumbo about these "uncanny" events. They liken this phenomenon to the sensitive and knowing way couples who
have been closely and happily married for many years so
often know just what the other feels or needs or wants. Their
exceptional identification gives twins an extra sensitivity to
each other's moods, permitting them to know much about
what the other is experiencing. These similar reactions may
hark back to the similar reactions and experiences they
shared in their earliest months and years: sadness when their
mother left, and joy when she returned, excitement when
they both saw and reached for new objects, etc. If, therefore,
as Burlingham explains, referring again to the young twins
under three in her study, ". . . one twin experiences a pleasure or pain the other lives through the same experience in
identification. It is this constant process of identification with
each other on the basis of similarity of emotional experience
which keeps identical twins 'identical' in spite of acquired
differences."[7]

Special Problems of Opposite-Sex Twins

Although opposite-sex twins have the same potential for
enduring ties and a special closeness, they also may have
their share of difficulties. There is a lovely alternate version
of the Narcissus myth offered in the *New Encyclopedia Brittanica* in which Narcissus pines away not by gazing at his
own image in the pool as most people remember, but, while
trying to console himself over the death of his adored twin
sister. ". . . his exact counterpart, he sat gazing into the spring
to recall her features by his own."[8]

In real life when one of the twins of the opposite sex
marries, occasionally the possessiveness and jealousy leaves
the single partner utterly dejected and lost. In one of her
poignant stories about village life in Ireland, published in *The
New Yorker* some years ago, Maeve Brennan tells of a woman
with other siblings who suffers bitter pangs of jealousy when
her thirty-seven-year-old twin, Martin, marries.

Not that I was ever jealous, Min thought. God forbid that I should encourage small thoughts in myself, but I couldn't help but despise Delia that day, the way she stood looking up at Martin as though she was ready to fall on her knees before him. [Then she thinks sadly later] The best part of their lives ended the day Martin met Delia. . . . From now on there would be nothing more between her and him than running into each other on the street once in a while.[9]

Another twin, Winifred, tells me of a totally different relationship shared with her brother Julius. "I had an older brother and sister, but between my two brothers I always like Julius better as a person. I was not aware that I felt this way because he was my twin, and I guess I'll never find out if this was so. Perhaps I thought of him just as a brother because we were raised more as individuals than as twins. But I did feel especially attached to him even though after adolescence we lived in different parts of the world. We and our families always kept in contact and frequently visited each other over the years."

Girl-boy pairs (as well as same-sex twins) sometimes develop strange fantasies about the nature and origin of their twinship. If one of the pair believes the other twin is more appealing—which belief may be fortified if this child sees or imagines that his or her parent leans toward the other—fantasies may arise that maybe the twin robbed the other in the womb of something he or she believes is lacking, size, brains, looks, a body part, or whatever. "I'm the rotten half of the apple," wailed one twin to her therapist at one of many sessions. The young woman felt her brother had it all over her and fantasized that he had gotten "more" in their mother's womb. The therapist thought her patient might want to hear some of the facts about twins. Very quietly and briefly she told her, "Each of you was a separate egg fertilized by two different sperm around the same time. There was plenty of room and nourishment for both of you in your mother's womb and you weren't deprived of anything there."

Such information is useful to all twins, adapted to the type and gender of twin they happen to be. A boy, in particular, may take a dim view, however, about the fact that "nobody got more" especially if his twin sister is taller than he. (Just before puberty, or right after, girls shoot up in height leaving their brothers behind, albeit temporarily. Few boys know that girls grow fast and mature earlier physically but that boys catch up in time.)

Apparently there can be some hazards for boy-girl twins not only for their sexual development but for their healthy emotional growth when they are repeatedly left together and also treated as "the twins." "Mother was very intuitive and wise," Winifred, the twin discussed previously, replied to another question about how she and Julius were raised. "As soon as possible, Mother saw to it that Julie and I had separate rooms, letting the others double up until we could move to larger quarters. She felt it of utmost importance that we each have physical privacy, a chance to develop our individual as well as our female and male selves. I think her treatment of us as unique personalities also helped us from feeling we were rivals."

Twins and Other Siblings

Any oldest, or even middle child, as already seen, faces a big letdown and much trouble when the next in line is born. But think of what he or she must feel when the "next" turns out to be twins. "Double trouble," "An invasion" are words used by some older sisters and brothers in expressing their early reactions. To make matters even worse, not only do these new sibs attract twice the amount of attention in the home but also outside the home.

"When I was four years old the twins arrived," Bert, a college junior, says. "All at once I became the invisible man. I felt terribly excluded when Mom took the three of us out, with the twins getting all the raves and acclaim, while I was totally ignored. Both Mom and Pop must have done a lot to help me feel that my place in their hearts was still there, because when I turned six I found the twins fun. I got real furious when my pals found it necessary to express a preference for either Alice or Paula. At that point I declared that I liked the other one best." Bert then tells of another older sibling, Oscar, from another family, who said that his twin sister and brother would gang up on him when he was in school since they were two years younger. "It was always two against one," Oscar had told him. "Years later, Oscar realized," Bert says, "that some of the flack they heaped on him was meant for each other, because when he went off to camp —a heaven for him—he heard that they really had let the other have it. Now they are seventeen but they still don't get along."

Twins, whether fraternal, identical, or girl-boy twins, can all enjoy a special relationship through understanding that *some* competition is inevitable and normal, and that the competitiveness can be expressed through sports, and even work, as long as it doesn't get nasty or become an overriding motive in life. They can also enjoy their relationship whether they have similar interests, tastes, careers, or go in totally different directions. While appreciating their closeness but leaving room for spaces, too, twins may enjoy their unity when they know that each one is a distinct person—a "me."

SPLITS IN
THE FAMILY

12

Broken Homes

A mother of three college-age children writes that when she was three-and-a-half and her brother, Jerry, was six, their father died suddenly. Her mother explained little to either of them about their father's disappearance, believing they were too young to comprehend. She and her brother were bewildered; they couldn't understand why their adored father had left them. The two also felt shut off from their mother, who was deeply immersed in her own grief and other problems. All of this had brought Jerry and her closer together. "We were each other's emotional anchors and protectors," she writes. "I recall—even to this day—that when I was about five, some bully started to shove Jerry around. In a fury, with all my strength I stamped my tiny foot, shod in white kid shoes, upon his toes, yelling, 'Don't you *dare* push my brother!' The boy was so taken aback that my brother had a chance to let him have it and he ran away like lightning."

Later, when she started dating, Jerry would give her boyfriends "a once over, warning me about those he thought were most likely to have their teeth kicked in later in life, and those who had possibilities of becoming real human beings." She indicated that Jerry had been almost a father to her and, today, although he and his family live in Texas, they call each other frequently. "Invariably, after inquiring about

Tom and our three kids," she adds, "Jerry will—of course, not literally—ask me if I've brushed my teeth that day. His solicitude fills my whole being with warmth and I'm right back in memory to those early days."

Two sisters whose mother died when they were four and five years of age became inseparable, and never expressed any of the usual sibling antagonisms during their growing years. If either was jealous of the other's place in their father's affections, it was never evident. Years later, as grown women, they took a trip together to visit him on his birthday. During their stay, several heated battles of words interrupted their usual harmony and one sister announced she was leaving. Their wise and knowing father, convinced that they all might profit by exploring possible reasons for these unexpected clashes, asked her to stay on. After much soul-searching, the young women began to realize that an early rivalry and jealousy had been withheld from consciousness until this particular reunion when some remark had triggered buried angers. As young children they had clung desperately to each other in mutual need and loneliness, unable to express any hostile feelings for fear of losing each other and their father, as well. They also may have believed, unconsciously, that their earlier jealousy and angry thoughts toward their mother had sent *her* away.

Relationships between Siblings
When a Parent Dies

These brief stories show how brothers and sisters are often united in a deeply moving way when a parent dies. Sharing a common plight, the children may turn to one another for support and comfort, each drawing on the other's strengths. The death of a parent may overwhelm the young child with shock, pain, bewilderment, helplessness, and yearning. Not understanding the permanence of death, the very young child tends to feel abandoned and longs for his or her parent's return. Since children under the age of six or so believe in the magic power of their thoughts, they may worry about those moments of anger when they entertained "bad" thoughts, wishing to get rid of their mother or father, and may believe now that those unfortunate wishes have come true. Older children may feel guilt over recalcitrant behavior shown while their lost parent was alive, and teenagers may be caught in a whirlpool of sad, guilty, and remorseful feelings as they recall how they struggled to free themselves from closeness to the parent now dead.

The children's need for reassurance and understanding comes at a time when a parent, grappling with his or her own pain, anger, and loneliness, may be unable to provide the sensitive care the children now need. Even later, when a parent is once again emotionally available to the children, they may have made attempts to master the pain of their loss together, trying to find relief from their distress. Brothers and sisters who are close in age may huddle together during and after such a loss and forge strong love bonds not easily broken. If there is a greater age difference, one, either girl or boy, may take on a substitute mother or father role. The sibs may draw from the good mothering and fathering of happier days, more as givers than receivers in their relationship to one other. Such a reversal of roles may be hard on the child because it leaves little freedom for the natural rivalry of "mine" and "yours." Still, some psychiatrists believe to pay this price may be worthwhile, because children who act as parents may be spared *some* of the pangs of their deprivation. The older sister or brother may become aware that feelings of caring and belonging still exist and have meaning, and this can deflect from, and modify, their sense of loss.

A divorced now remarried fashion director of a women's magazine tells me how she and her sister, at twelve and ten, bonded together for solace and comfort when their adored father died. But they also knew that their mother, beset with periodic bouts of alcoholism, would not be able to meet the emotional needs of their four-year-old brother. Putting aside their "petty jealousies," as this eldest sister tells it, "Each day we took turns after school to play with Randy and read to him. At night we cuddled and soothed him and often gave him back rubs. As often as we could, we took Randy along with us on outings with our friends, and bought him a dog with our own savings. We felt we were more of a family than ever—our ties reinforced forever." Luckily for them, their Uncle Ben, who lived nearby, provided the three with male companionship and encouragement. "Ellen, Randy, and I have been especially devoted and tuned into each other's vibes since those days, and we'll fly to each other's side whenever one of us is in trouble or need."

Without the presence of a kindly, gentle, guiding adult, children who have not yet reached middle or sometimes even late adolescence—still grappling with the normal problems of growing up added to their loss—may have grave difficulties in taking on the responsibility of being a mothering or fathering sister or brother. Under the worst of circumstances their ambivalent feelings toward, and treatment of, their younger sibs may alternate from extreme indulgence to uncontrolled hostility. But others, who were fortified emotionally through happy early years with their parents, may now be stable and responsible. They may go to heroic lengths to hold the family together after the death of a parent. It was this way with Stella, as described by a close friend, Louise.

Stella and Louise grew up in Darien, Connecticut. When the two met, Stella was six and the eldest of four children. Louise remembers Stella's mother "as a beautiful, warm, graceful, and much loved woman who ran a huge estate with gorgeous gardens. She had all the worldly possessions anyone could want, yet remained unspoiled. Her children adored her and she loved them. The youngest, a little girl, was only two years old when this lovely woman was stricken with cancer and died within eight months. A big blow and a total shock to the children."

Without a mother's influence and love, or even that of a substitute mother—the servants were unable to supply this substitute love, and their busy father sought consolation outside of the home—the home began to fall apart. By then Stella was nine. The lack of a parenting person was particularly hard on the two middle boys, age seven and six. The oldest boy went berserk at school one day and was hospitalized for several months, during which he received intensive psychotherapy. Try as she could, with all her efforts to mother, Stella was unable to meet all of her younger brothers' and sister's needs, and the situation deteriorated. Several years later their father married a much younger woman who had no control over or effect on the children. They resented her presence and her strict ways, and became rebellious. Stella continued to remain the steady child she had always been, never lost her temper and, at age twelve, was as loving as she could be to her younger sibs. However, her father began to drink, lost a large part of his money, and died soon after of a heart attack.

"Once more the children suffered a great loss," Louise goes on, "and the stepmother had no use for the youngsters so the family was split up." One aunt took the youngest girl; the two boys were sent to a foster home in a nearby city; and Stella lived with another aunt and uncle. She visited her sister twice a week and brothers weekly. By now her only goal was to bring her family back together again. As soon as she reached her eighteenth birthday, she found herself a good job, rented an apartment, went to court to get custody of the children, and succeeded. The two boys had a number of behavior problems, and took out a lot of their anger and frustration on Stella. But somehow her steadiness and love helped them to regain some of the sense of trust they had developed in early childhood. "At this point," Louise concludes, "Stella is about to marry a marvelous man, a history professor who will take the children under his wing until they are able to manage on their own in a few years. I have to add, however, that one of the boys is in therapy. But everyone wonders what would have become of this family had it not been for Stella."

Relationships between Siblings
When Parents Divorce

Peter, a pre-medical student, remembers that when his parents divorced it was a great relief to him and his two older brothers not to hear their mother and father shouting, arguing, and fighting any longer. "Still, when they finally announced their decision to divorce, our whole world seemed to collapse," he says. He was eight, his brothers, eleven and ten. "Many of our parents' friends were divorced and we took divorce for granted as a way of life that happened in other homes, but when it struck *ours, wham,* it sure upset us. Who were we going to live with? Who did we love better, Mom or Dad? When we knew that Dad was going to leave home and we'd stay with Mom we worried about whether we'd be seeing him often, and if he did see us, would we have to take turns to see him? Who was right or wrong? Mom or Dad? Who should we side with?" They were caught up in a vortex of conflicting feelings and loyalties. Despite the divorce, their parents continued to argue about the children, and were, in consequence, "at each other's throats most of the time." When Gene was fifteen, he decided to live with his father; the other two preferred to stay with their mother. "Things were never quite the same with us and Gene after that," Peter explained.

Divorce, like the death of a parent, is an upheaval and shock for children. They are thrust into a situation not of their own making, yet they often blame themselves for the disaster. Divorce may aggravate resentful feelings among sisters and brothers, or it may bring about a new closeness as with the crisis of death. As with death children may react to the splitup of their parents by feeling that they have been punished for their "bad" thoughts and actions, responsible for the breakup. If they'd been better behaved maybe it wouldn't have happened. Teen-agers often feel doubly enmeshed in guilt and conflicting loyalties caused by their reawakened possessive attachment to their opposite-sex parent. Most adults whose parents were divorced when they were children admit they had secretly hoped in those days that their parents would get together again and remarry.

As sisters and brothers begin to rearrange their inner and outer lives, their relationship to one another cannot help but be affected. Their hurt and sense of rejection, and their mother's or father's own feelings of hurt and anger, bitterness, and desolation are bound to take a toll with sisters and brothers. Especially vulnerable now to signs of being overlooked by a parent, all the normal sibling jealousies frequently become exacerbated. Several adults told me that when a sister or brother was allowed to stay up later at night or was granted privileges, they regarded it as further "proof" that their parent preferred this other child.

"At first things were hard on me, but even harder on Dot and Brian who seemed in constant vigilance, looking over their shoulders to be sure each was getting her or his fair portion of my love and not the short end of the stick," says a divorced mother, describing the early postdivorce days with her young children.

Other divorced fathers (and mothers, if the fathers have custody of the children) tell of their children's reactions on those first reunions. One of them says, "At first I felt I should give the kids a round of treats—dinners out, circus, ballgames, movies, museums, and all that jazz—but my three youngsters would scrap and one would say, 'I want to do this,' another, 'I want to do that.' And if I did 'this' rather than 'that' the other would cry and say, 'You love Joe more than me.' I soon decided it would be better for all of us to have quiet and relaxed afternoons and evenings at my apartment where we could have some time to talk, fix meals together, and watch TV."

Another became a sort of visiting Santa Claus. If the sailboat he bought Ralph cost a few dollars more or looked bigger than the game he bought Jenny, the girl seemed to suffer under the false impression that the costlier object symbolized more love. Such distortions of reality can occur at such times since children often equate money and gifts with love. Other part-time parents as well as at-home parents are able to help the sisters and brothers avoid this trap, or extricate them from it.

"We were lucky," a young research chemist comments, "because we had none of this. Our mother and father had many open, honest dialogues with us and gave us even more of themselves than before the divorce. They each were sincerely and deeply interested in our lives and problems and we never felt that material offerings or privileges had anything to do with the quality or quantity of the love we each received. The four of us knew we still had a loving mother and father even if they weren't married any more."

Brothers and sisters often siphon off some of their anger and guilt onto each other. A thirty-three-year-old divorcée went to a child psychiatrist shortly after her marriage broke up to get some help on the trouble that had arisen between her five-and-a half-year-old son, Ricky, and her ten-year-old Gus.

After several sessions of talking about Ricky and Gus and herself, the doctor explained that Ricky was still in the throes of his possessive attachment to her, and in one way felt glad that his father was out of the home. "Ricky probably felt he could have you all to himself now," the doctor suggested.

"But," the divorcée explains, "it didn't work out that

way because I was unhappy to begin with and preoccupied with my problems, and, besides, as Dr. B. pointed out, Ricky had to share me with Gus, who in a way seemed like a father to him—a double rival."

The psychiatrist seemed to feel that the boy was also unhappy because he still loved and needed his father (even though the father had tried to poison Ricky's mind against his mother). In addition, or because of all his confusions and mixed feelings, the boy felt guilty, and the guilt made him feel angry. "Since Gus wasn't his *real* Daddy, Ricky made him the target for all his misery, guilt, and rage." The divorcée was amazed that when Ricky would start to hit and attack Gus, Gus quietly refused to counterattack. Like a "good" father, he managed to hold little Rick firmly in check, warding off his blows. "Somehow," Dr. B. told her, "Gus seems to vaguely comprehend and empathize with Ricky's pain. He can handle his own unhappiness because he is now at an age where he no longer needs you in the way Ricky does, and instead he is putting his all into his school work." Soon after, with Dr. B.'s help, this formerly distressed woman understood even more and things began to simmer down.

Another cause for bitter fighting among sisters and brothers during the divorce crisis, says Ann S. Kliman, director of the Situational Crisis Service of the Center for Preventive Psychiatry in White Plains, New York, is "polarization." "If parents continue to be loving parents to their children, the siblings are apt to identify with the loving qualities of their mother and father, and care for, and look after each other. But if the youngsters became pawns or weapons in a tug-of-war between their parents, they are apt to identify with these parents in the same fashion." In these loyalty splits, Ann Kliman explained in a talk with me, the "goodies" are ranged on one side and the "baddies" on the other. One child lines up with and represents one parent, and the other takes the part of the other parent. Then they may engage in free-for-all fights over who is "right" and who is "wrong."

Ann Kliman recalls a family with a nineteen-year-old son and two daughters, age fourteen and thirteen. "After much bitter haranguing between the parents, a divorce took place. The father was rather irresponsible, although he cared for his children. The mother was a responsible, caring parent but somewhat rigid." The three children were angry at both parents, yet, as Ann Kliman describes it, "the *overt* rage erupted between the fourteen-year-old girl and her older brother. The two were actually reenacting the marital situation, identifying with the *worst* aspects of *both* parents."

In one divorce described by Ann Kliman, carried out in a more "civilized" manner, both the mother and father were sensitive to the children's anguish and pain. During arguments they reassured the children that they were having grown-up problems having nothing to do with *them.* The elder sister of seven "was obviously modeling herself after her caring mother and father." Her demanding four-year-old sister often clung to her, or grabbed her toys, or even the French fries from her plate. The older sister would be irritated but then would apologize with feeling. She seemed to have understood her sister's distress. She heard her mother respond to similar episodes by saying, "I know you're trying to fill up your lonely, empty feelings inside. Many children get grabby and greedy when they feel scared and lonely." As Ann Kliman puts it, "The mother's empathic responses gave her youngster a chance to acknowledge her need for extra loving and find more appropriate ways of expressing this need, such as 'Mommy, read me a story, please.' "[1]

Many children of divorced parents, now grown women and men, say emphatically that the warmth, empathy, and patience of their mother or father—or both—helped them to overcome their unhappiness and grow in health and strength. Unless one parent denigrated the other, forcing the siblings into the painful situation of having to take sides, thereby polarizing their loyalties and projecting their angry feelings onto each other, most sisters and brothers come to see that they are in the same boat, going over the same rough waves. They are able to row together, bolstering each other up as they work toward resolving their conflicts and rebuilding their lives.

13

Stepsiblings and Half-Siblings

"We had barely caught our breath after Mother and Father divorced, when Father suddenly married a woman he'd known for a long time—a widow with kids around the same age as Anita, who was eleven at the time, and me, nine." Debbie, a young photographer went on to tell me that she and her sister felt their father had betrayed their mother and worried about how this marriage would affect them. Would they be lost in the shuffle? Would they have to divide their time with their father on weekends with the other kids? "These and other worries made us hate that family sight unseen. But, later, we discovered that Elsie, our stepmother, was really a good person and sensitive to our predicament." Susie and Matt, their stepsister and stepbrother, looked forward eagerly to the weekend visits that made the girls feel they had another home. Their father took them out a lot during their first visits to his new home, "until we had to *ask* him to include Sue and Matt."

Things were not always so simple for other adults who speak of their childhood introduction to new step-relatives.

Once more those issues of conflicting loyalties were frequently played out on stepsisters and brothers.

"Sometimes," observes Lucille Stein, a New York City therapist, "the child or children may continue to feel angry that Mommy could have thrown over Daddy and fastened onto another man. Or, a boy may feel, 'I'm living with Mommy and glad about that,' but also feel guilty that he was glad on account of his other feelings about Daddy." In both cases, Lucille Stein explains, the stepparent or stepsiblings frequently become the recipient of the child's anger, because negative feelings are often heaped onto someone other than the person for whom they are intended. The child may think, or say, "You aren't my *real* sister (or brother), and I don't have to like you." Or, the child feels, "You're not part of my family. Why do I have to be nice to you?" which implies a nonacceptance of the changed family situation. On the other hand, Lucille Stein continues, "the children of both marriages may become allies because here's someone around your own age who has shared the same uprooting and sadness of divorce. Both sets of siblings may have felt pushed aside and left out, and now they find they can form a new league against their parents. There might be a sense of relief. 'I've got a pal now. Things are going to be better and we'll work it out together.' "[1]

Problems among Siblings from Different Sets of Homes

The first meetings between brothers and sisters from stepfamilies are often full of suspicion and distrust, but sometimes there is cautious appraisal and even tenuous approaches toward friendship. They are opposite teams—the Home Team and the Visiting Team. When one set of sibs is younger, say, four and six, and the other set, older, say, twelve and twelve and fifteen, tension may be replaced by curiosity and even excitement.

Time and sorting out are needed for inner and outer adjustments. The differences in lifestyles may be great. As one father comments, "I'm a Conservative observant Jew, my wife is Protestant; my children who visit us on holidays now celebrate Christmas and have learned to like plum pudding and apple pie, while my stepchildren celebrate Chanukah and have taken to gefilte fish, bagels, and lox."

In mixed marriages, stepchildren need to learn how to accept not only each other but each other's church or synagogue affiliations and beliefs—not always easy.

Other adults mention different obstacles. One father of six children had been an only child. When, as a child, he visited his father on weekends, he was nearly overwhelmed at first by three stepbrothers and stepsister. Never having had to share his father before with other children, all at once he had to adjust to his new stepmother and to her four children. His stepbrothers and stepsister came to his aid, however. Later he found out that his stepmother had asked them to welcome him to their home as they would a newcomer to school. "Finally," he concludes, "I came to enjoy being a part of a large family, feeling less isolated and lonely. I looked forward with pleasant anticipation to my visits knowing I would have ready-made playmates. Since those days, even to now, I consider my stepsiblings as real brothers and sister."

If the Home Team has to double up on visits from their stepsibs, sharing their room space, they may feel invaded. As one down-to-earth therapist suggests, "Children who resent making room for their visiting stepsiblings may not mind the loss or privacy as much as the fact that this superficial loss may represent sharing Stepfather and Mommy with the Visiting Team."

As in all matters concerning human beings, those who were given a chance to air their gripes before they became grudges may gradually have seen "the other side" and noticed through open discussions that all youngsters have common needs and feelings much like their own.

Anne W. Simon adds this bit of wisdom from her book, *Stepchild in the Family*:

. . . if a child observes his mother or father becoming a friendly stepparent to another child and finds such a relationship himself, he can begin to see the strengths in his new kind of family. When honestly regarded, the complications become an asset. There is not much room for fantasy and disappointed dreams in the hardy climate of the 'She's *my* mother,' 'Well, he's *my* father' dialogue. A new kind of peace can happen."[2]

"My chief worry," a young mother recalls, "was, what goes on with Dad and my stepsisters after my visit with him is over? After all, he spends every single day of the week with them and surely shows interest, affection, and concern for them. So, I felt I had to outdo them and be 'better' and 'smarter' and altogether more appealing than the others. It put me on edge and my jealousy was felt by my stepsisters. Until I felt surer of my father, my stepmother, stepsibs, and myself, my stepsisters and I kept out of each other's way."

And what happens to those on the Home Team? Aren't they jealous of their stepfather's and mother's attention to the visiting sibs? In their book *Part-Time Father,* Edith Atkin and Estelle Rubin describe such a situation:

A mother of two sons told how her older boy, age thirteen, sensitively withdrew when her husband's boys visited, allowing the father to be alone with his own children. However, her younger son, age eight, who enjoyed being with his step-father, resented not being included in the father's outings with his own children. These authors suggest that a father could bide his time until everyone felt more at ease, and *then* include the other children in shared experiences.[3]

Different Lifestyles in Different Homes

A school counselor describes another common situation. Jessie, age sixteen, poured out her complaints to the counselor in one long breath. "Those kids at Amy's [her stepmother] don't have to make their beds. They are real slobs and leave their clothes and junk all over the place, and, sure, they are living it up in a huge mansion with servants, and have a swimming pool and tennis court." The counselor discovered that Jessie actually enjoyed the luxuries of her weekends there, but also felt guilty about enjoying herself as well as being resentful, because, as Jessie had explained, holding back tears, "At home, Davy, Mom, and I do all the heavy work and we scrounge around for every cent while Dad spends his money on the other kids." It so happened that Jessie's father had married a wealthy divorcée with two teenage girls. Her father tried to explain that he wasn't giving his stepdaughters more than his own children; the money wasn't his, but belonged to his wife. He was sending his own family all he could. But, the counselor observed, one of the underlying problems that made Jessie seek help was her great difficulty in reconciling herself to her father's remarriage. And, of course, she was jealous of the stepsisters who were so much a part of his life.

It is easy to see, then, how vast economic differences between stepfamilies that *seem* to pit one set of siblings against the other may be, at times, precipitating factors that set off deeper fears and unresolved conflicts.

Nonetheless, some not-to-be-overlooked realities—differences in values, standards, and discipline in one home as compared to another—may cause strife among the young. One home is freer and more flexible about rules and regulations. Another home demands more of the children and insists on regular hours for bedtime, meals, and for watching TV. "I secretly gloated," a woman told me, "when my visiting stepsister protested to Mother and my stepfather, 'But at home my mother lets me stay up until 11' and 'I don't have to make my bed at home.' Then my mother replied kindly that the rules in this home were different."

To avoid chaos and greater resentments, some mutually agreed upon ground rules can be set up. Both sets of children may feel more at home and equal and can gripe in unison over the common "injustices."

Naturally, many remarried couples have said that their greatest fear was that their marriage would suffer if the stepchildren didn't hit it off. But it usually is the other way around. As Lucille Duberman notes in her study *The Reconstructed Family: A Study of Remarried Couples and Their Children*, if the new couple is really happy together, their happiness is apt to spill over to the stepchildren; and they invariably get to like each other.[4]

A TV film editor says that her father and stepmother's home had been such a happy one that when she was thirteen and her brother fifteen they decided to live with them and their stepsibs. By that time their mother was remarried and starting a new family.

Such optimism, however, must be tempered by the fact that, often, skeletons in the closet of the children's former lives keep rattling around and interfering with their relationships to the *best* of stepparents and stepsibs. Miserable experiences and conflicts in their past lives may have left unhealed wounds. An unhappy child coming into a happy home, or one who is visited by a stepsibling coming from a home where the atmosphere is warm and accepting, may feel jealous and resentful. No matter how friendly the stepsibs, such unhappy youngsters—unless helped by therapy—often remained aloof, uninvolved with, or even antagonistic to the other children.

Relationships between Stepsiblings Who Live in the Same Home

When all stepsiblings live under the same roof, because of custody arrangements or remarriage after the death of one parent, all of the problems are accentuated, certainly in the beginning, at least. Yet after difficult initial adjustments, stepsisters and brothers frequently reap permanent benefits. Lucille Duberman found in her study that of forty-five families with two sets of children from former marriages, "When both sets of children lived in the same house, the relations between them were more likely to be 'excellent' than if they lived in different houses."[5]

In these completely merged families, there is a good deal of leveling off of differences in lifestyles, as occurred in TV's *The Brady Bunch.* Scrapping notwithstanding, stepsisters and brothers often build up a sense of kinship, a clan feeling, because there is and always will be a strong urge in children to feel they have roots and "belong" to a real family. Camaraderie grows; both sets of siblings can now identify more closely with each other.

Some shifts in the sibling hierarchy take place as one child is compelled to relinquish—seldom happily—the position as eldest in the family. The loss in seniority may be a matter of only a week or two. The former youngest may not mind surrendering the place as youngest since now the *other* has to go to bed earlier and have fewer privileges. They have now got up a rung on the hierarchal ladder.

Tensions and bruised feelings usually appear all around when couples declare, "It's *your* child's fault," or if a stepparent bends over backward not to interfere when the stepchild attacks his or her *own* child. Youngsters thrive on the kind of sensitive concern—which makes them feel more protected and secure—when the remarried couple adopts an attitude of "Let's try to see together what is causing the friction between our kids."

Other families tell of reducing dissensions through holding family forums. Psychologist Dr. Stevanne Auerbach, consultant for Parent and Child Care Resources, a San Francisco organization, used a forum with her five-year-old daughter and three older stepchildren. The children settled disputes among themselves through a family council, set up once a week, usually after dinner "when everyone was feeling good. As we all sat together, we found out what the others felt, needed, and wanted from each other and from us. They saw that we were trying to be fair since we never took sides, but just helped the discussion to move along. At one time my seven-year-old stepdaughter had been teasing my five-year-old and had been impatient with her because she had been unable to do things that she, the older one, managed easily. Through discussion in the council my seven-year-old step-child learned more about what one could expect of a child of five. The older youngster also saw then that I wasn't baby-ing or 'spoiling' my daughter—as she had thought—and it made both girls feel better." Dr. Auerbach adds, however, that while each sister and brother needs some space and time, particularly children who share a room, a wife and husband also need space for their own relationship—time away from their children and some intervals for each other.[6]

And what happens to the close and loving, slowly but securely formed relationship between stepsiblings when their parent and stepparent divorce once again? For it does happen. Sometimes, if the ex-couple remains cordial, the stepsisters and brothers keep in touch with each other—in some cases throughout adulthood. Under other circum-stances, their relationship is ripped apart, either because of hostility between the couple, passed onto the children, or merely because one of them moves away. "I was an only child," Sylvia, a college student, reveals, "and when my di-vorced mother remarried, I was six, and rather lonely. At first I was guarded when my stepfather, Chuck—who had cus-tody of his only child, Grace, two years older than I—moved into our home. Soon after, however, she and I became 'bosom' friends. We couldn't wait until shcool was out so we could compare notes and be with each other. We were sisters in the deepest sense of the word. It was almost a tragedy for both of us when Mother and Chuck divorced. We wept a lot over our separation. Grace and I tried to keep up with each other but Chuck moved away and there went my sister. Years after, we somehow met again and broke down and cried with joy and sorrow. Now we at least write to one another and are trying to arrange it so our paths will cross more often."

The New Extended Family

More so today than in the last generation of children whose parents divorced, an entirely "new kind of an old kind" of extended family is emerging. As one woman puts it, "My granddaughter, Amy, age seven, is living in the best of all possible worlds. Alma, my divorced daughter, is sharing her life with a good man who adores his 'illegitimate' stepdaughter (of course I'd like to see the 'couple' marry). Amy's father, for whom I have the utmost respect, loves her deeply. He is remarried and has not only a wife who is enchanted with Amy, but their three-year-old child considers her his own property. And you won't believe this, but his parents-in-law have taken to Amy too. They are 'Gram and Gramp' to her."

The ability of grandparents (and other kith and kin) to become havens of comfort and providers of emotional sustenance to children whose parents are divorced or remarried, often gives them that much needed feeling of sameness and continuity. Yet sometimes a stepgrandchild is ignored or even rejected by the grandparents. An accountant told me: "I felt left out because it was obvious that Jacob and Jonathan's Granny felt quite differently about them than she did about me, and at the time neither Mom nor Dad had prepared me to expect this. I kind of thought of her as my granny too because three of my own grandparents had died long ago and my remaining grandmother was far away in a nursing home. I deeply envied my stepbrothers and felt sorry for myself."

When caring and sympathetic grandparents have really accepted their new daughter- or son-in-law, they do respond to the family cohesiveness, and warmly welcome the stepsiblings into the wider family circle. Even those who live some distance away never fail to include their stepgrandchildren on the telephone after speaking to their own. Or, they keep up a correspondence with them. In some families, stepsibs may have eight grandparents instead of four.

San Francisco radio commentator and interviewer Owen Spann wrote a book with his wife, Nancie Spann, *Your Child? I Thought It Was My Child!* Owen and Nancie each had two sons and a daughter from previous marriages. The two had just returned from a trip to Egypt:

Chris ran out the door. "Oh, hi, Mom and O. Welcome to the world travelers. Grandma's on the telephone."

"Grandma who?" we asked.

"Grandma Ruth," he answered.

OWEN: That's my mother. No relation to the Anderson kids but very much a part of our elongated family and very much an accepted grandma to them as well as to her own.

NANCIE: Last spring during Ellen's stay with us, my mother happened to be visiting too. Early one morning I walked into Nana's room to find her and her stepgranddaughter cuddled in bed together talking in intimate terms. Would a stranger to the scene have known they were not related?[7]

Stepsisters and brothers who have found loving members in the extended family are truly fortunate.

Boy-Girl Relationships between Stepsiblings

Opposite-sex siblings often develop friendlier relationships than same-sex sibs, unless they continue to be angry at their parents' remarriage.

Less rivalry and competitiveness may exist between cross-sex than same-sex siblings, unless, of course, a stepmother or stepfather shows favoritism to a child of either sex.

The feelings of friendliness and interest may increase if sexual interest or attraction is sparked between boy and girl when they first meet. The incest taboo may be lowered since stepbrothers and sisters are not blood relatives and they know it. More often than not, these initially sexually tinged feelings are transformed into closeness, loyalty, sisterly and brotherly love.

Reports from several distressed stepparents, from books on the subject of remarriage and stepchildren, and from personal memories of adults who once were in this situation, reveal that sex play, romantic involvements, and even marriages sometimes take place among stepchildren.

One needs to take a sober look at these reports and define and separate sex play, erotic or romantic attachments, and marriage. How old were the children when the families merged? Were these visiting stepchildren, or stepchildren all growing up in the same home?

Occasional sex play or experimentation is of course usually a part of a child's growing-up experiences, and may involve a sister or brother or a young playmate. It could also include a stepsibling. Just as with children who are blood sisters and brothers, there is a cause for worry only if intensity and repetitiveness is attached to such play, or if an older child involves a much younger one.

By and large when stepsisters and brothers who grew up from childhood as a family become adolescents, they move out of the nest in their search for sexual partners and marriage. Sometimes sensual hugs, kisses, fondling, flirting between stepsister and brother who grow up together indicate that some distorting unconscious messages are at play interfering with the youngsters' healthy emotional growth. The adolescent girl or boy may be acting out on the stepsibling an unconscious fantasy about their opposite-sex stepparent, or even one built around their own parent of the opposite sex.

When families join together during or just before their children's adolescence, a romantic relationship can occasionally develop, for quite realistic reasons.

A remarried couple with a combined family of five children noticed signals between two of their teen-agers that made them uncomfortable. In this case, the remarriage had taken place only three years previously. The mother tells it this way: "One day we followed our intuition and came upon my fifteen-year-old Joe and Dave's fourteen-year-old Terry on her bed in various stages of undress, fondling each other passionately. We were quite upset but didn't want to make a federal case out of it. We carefully explained that we had become a family; their intimacy was confusing and destructive to family life. There were plenty of girls and boys outside of the home with whom they could form relationships, and with whom they could fall in love. Fortunately, their attraction for each other had not yet taken root, and to the best of our knowledge this incident was never repeated. Now they are adults. Joe is married, and Terry living with a young man she hopes to marry someday."

Even though we know this *isn't* incest, sexual attachments and behavior between adolescent stepchildren have always confronted and violated our sense of the incest taboo. The stepparents above were trying to set up standards and some restrictions in their home to protect the family and to promote the choice of more appropriate relationships for their children and stepchildren.

A slightly different story is told by one father of his visiting son and stepdaughter. "When I married Gail's mother, Gail was a very mature thirteen, and my son Bob, fifteen. The two liked and admired each other, sharing a number of interests, especially a love of baroque music. They were good friends until Bob went off to college three years later. When he returned for visits, they fell in love and made plans to marry in a couple of years. We begged them to reconsider, look around further in the larger world and not make any plans now. But they loved each other and finally married. We can't explain exactly why, but we were quite embarrassed, and regretful too, but they seem so happy that we've become reconciled."

Anthropologist Paul Bohannan sums up the many confusions that exist in these new relationships among stepchildren, suggesting that "the axioms on which law and beliefs are based say that these persons are not 'related' to one another." He writes, in *Divorce and After:*

> Americans are struggling to create norms in all these "new" relationships; it is my own opinion that nothing short of a presidential blue-ribbon committee to consider matters, with a widespread —indeed propagandistic—public relations coverage of the results can lead to new and approved patterns of family organization. The present situation approaches chaos, with each individual set of families having to work out its own destiny without any realistic guidance.[8]

A recently remarried couple with several about-to-become adolescent stepchildren feel that they certainly would never spy on their children but rather would keep a cool eye on what their relationships seem to be and in what direction they are going. And if anything untoward should happen they would at least *try* to respond to the situation itself, rather than to their own fears and taboos, and to handle it rationally. If the situation seemed beyond them, they would seek professional advice.

Half-Siblings

In addition to the jealous fears of every child upon the arrival of a new baby in the family, the stepchild's fears of displacement are further intensified when a half-sibling is born. More so for the visiting stepchild who can't fully participate in either the fun of observing the baby each day, or helping to nurture it at times. They are not able to protect their territorial rights to their father's or mother's love while they are away. How can stepsiblings avoid jealousy? They know that their half-sibling shares the same two parents while they belong to only one of them. The other stepsiblings often find, however, that they are on more equal ground, with something quite tangible in common—even if at first only mutual envy of the new baby.

Such setbacks are usually only temporary. After they come to accept the remarriage of their parent, they are more likely to accept the new baby, too. With the birth of a half-sister or brother, the rifts, the pain, and suffering of recent years seem to recede further into the past. The presence of the new child gives real evidence that this marriage is meant to endure; therefore, the stepsiblings' own feelings of security are strengthened. The half-blood sister or brother may actually become the link that joins both sets of siblings together as a family.

"The new child usually makes the family real now to both sets of siblings," says Lucille Stein. "A child could think somewhat along these lines, 'We weren't a real family before the baby came to join us.' " But now the child has become the link "between all of us; my connection with *that* Mommy (or Daddy) is through the fact that this new baby has some of *me* in him, some of that *Mommy,* some of my *Daddy* and some of those other children."[9]

Strong bonds and lasting attachments can develop between half-siblings who are fairly close in age. Ann Kliman tells a touching story of a thirteen-year-old boy who tried to help his unhappy younger half-brother, age nine, when their mother was divorcing for the second time (the first time for the younger boy, whose father was going to leave the home). "I know how you feel," the older child said, tenderly, "I remember how *I* felt when Mommy and *my* Daddy got divorced. I was so *scared.* But now every Saturday I see my Daddy. It's hard for you to know this, but I didn't lose my Daddy, and you're not going to lose yours either."[10]

A restaurant owner says that when she was born she already had a ten-year-old half-sister, the daughter of her father by a previous marriage. She speaks of her with great affection. "We all adored Kathy. I was the first half-sibling for her, then came my brother and sister. I always went to Kathy rather than to Mother with my problems and it was she who calmed me down when I was upset. She listened carefully and sympathetically to my tales of woe, told me the facts of life since Mother never offered information on the subject, and as far as I was concerned she was my real sister."

While the relationships within a family that include a half-sibling may not always have been as supportive as those described, angers, jealousies, and resentments invariably are reduced when each of the children becomes sure that individual voices will not be drowned out by the others. Regardless of "who's who" in the various combinations of blood, step, or half-siblings, basic human feelings remain the same, and the need all children have for closeness, self-validation, friendship, and love—when met—usually overrides much of the tensions created by their new family setup.

IV

SPECIAL PROBLEMS OF ADULT BROTHERS AND SISTERS

14
Marriages and the Wider Family

When a sister or brother first moves away from home, such as going off to college, along with the excitement and adventurous feeling of exploring the world there is often a pull backward too. The young person may, at first, have some feelings of trepidation—not shown on the surface—to remain secure within the family's protective embrace.

As for the remaining sibs at home, a way of life ends, the sameness has gone. A mother of eight children gave me an example: "All of us felt a pall; a sense of gloom descended over our home when Tricia, our eldest, went away to the state university." An agricultural student recalls, "When I was seventeen, right after Kate had left for college, Bob got married, and I not only felt deserted but was put into the awkward position of being the 'only' child at home." The one or ones left behind feel a sense of loss and tend to miss the past status quo, which is now often idealized, and frequently they wish something would cause the brother or sister to return.

Psychologists Stephen Bank and Michael Kahn relate a boy's reaction when his older brother took off for college. "I had a terrible lump in my throat when he got on the bus," the boy said. "I felt that I had lost my best friend. In fact, I think he really is my best friend. After all, who else is there to shoot the bull with around the house? We used to double date and do all kinds of things together. . . . I haven't felt the same since he left." As these psychologists suggest, "The separation of siblings through life-cycle events can remove the buffer that the remaining sibling has between himself and his parents."[1]

Sense of Loss When a Sibling Marries

In Louisa M. Alcott's *Little Women,* Jo, a year younger than Meg, seventeen, is distressed when she realizes that her sister is considering marriage to John Brooke. She declares unhappily, "I just wish I could marry Meg myself and keep her safe in the family." When it finally becomes clear that Meg will indeed marry, Jo talks to her friend Laurie: " 'You can't know how hard it is for me to give up Meg,' she said with a little quiver in her voice." And later, " 'It can never be the same again. I've lost my dearest friend,' sighed Jo."[2]

Do Jo's words seem hopelessly outdated? A present-day Jo, Eunice, at sixteen is weeping at her older sister's wedding. She asks her plaintively, "Will you come back to live with us if you get divorced?"

Other contemporary sisters often feel much like Jo and Eunice. "Will you still tell me everything after you're married?" a young woman, older than the bride, asked her sister, hopefully. "I know nothing will *ever* be the same between us after you're married," wailed another, one of four sisters, when her closest sister announced her intention of marrying a man she had been living with for some time. This young woman burst into tears after the wedding was over and the young couple had departed on their honeymoon.

Still others may deny any sense of loss. Candice put up a good front when her only sister married. "Well, at least she won't be stealing my clothes any more." Or, as a senior in high school put it, "Now I can have my room all to myself."

Brothers too may feel an emotional jolt at first when a

sister becomes a bride or a brother marries. One twenty-three-year-old had a sister, four years older, who was almost a mother to him. The young man had never had any serious attachments to a girl before, but when he learned of his sister's engagement, he almost immediately became involved with a woman five years his senior, a divorcée with two children, and moved into her home.

Those, of course, whose siblings have long moved away from home to lead independent lives may find that the impact of their first separation and loss of intimacy has been somewhat resolved by the time of a sister's or brother's marriage.

Jealousy at Marriage and After

Marriages of siblings can also feed competition in families where competitiveness was never alleviated. It is not unusual to hear a younger sister declare smugly, "Well, I married *first*" (or better, richer, or whatever). Another sister may remark, "You married first, but I produced the first grandchild." Again, this may give further proof that the sibs are still at it trying to gain "first place" with Mommy by presenting her with this unparalleled gift.

Another sister, whose mother had disapproved of her living with a man for several years, was denied the pleasure of wearing her mother's wedding dress. It hurt. Her younger sister was given this honor. But since the eldest sister's wedding was lavish and the younger sibling's wedding was simple, the two have battled for years over who "had it best."

Ordinarily, when siblings become older and their lives fairly well shaped or settled (or after divorces), they tend to rediscover some of the old intimacies, and the jealousies tend to fade away. Margaret Mead speaks to this point as she shows how sisters become closer as they grow older. She writes, in *Blackberry Winter: My Earlier Years:*

Sisters, while they are growing up, tend to be very rivalrous and as young mothers they are given to continual rivalrous comparisons of their several children. But once the children grow older, sisters draw closer together and often, in old age, they become each other's chosen and most happy companions. In addition to their shared memories of childhood, and of their relationships to each other's children, they share memories of the same home, the same homemaking style, and the small prejudices about housekeeping that carry echoes of their mother's voice as she admonished them, "Never fill the tea-kettle from the hot-water faucet," and "Wash the egg off the silver spoons at once," . . . But above all, perhaps sisters who have grown up close to one another know how their daydreams have been interwoven with their life experiences.[3]

Margaret Mead then tells, touchingly, how her ninety-five-year-old grandmother, gay and aware, still laments that "her sister, Emily, my mother, is not with her to share her last years."

Marriages: Siblings and Sibling In-Laws

When sisters and brothers have had fundamentally sound and caring relationships—notwithstanding the fights of their childhood, their different lifestyles or values—their marriage partners are apt to be warmly and wholeheartedly accepted into the family fold. In the words of one sister, "I was so happy when Tom and Jean found each other. I loved Jean from the start for having had the good sense and sensitivity to appreciate my brother's wonderful qualities. I knew during the years they lived together before their marriage that if he loved her she must be a swell person, too."

Sisters- and brothers-in-law (or vice versa) often become like one family, particularly if they live nearby—see each other and their offspring frequently, discuss and offer suggestions on problems concerning their children, friends, work, and aging parents. A sister and brother and mutual spouses sometimes take vacations together, and, while they may spat (more likely the sister and brother!) just as husband and wife may spat over where to go and what to do that day, many enjoy these shared holidays sufficiently to repeat them.

In the words of a single sister, "I never had the courage to go off on a trip abroad by myself, and knew I'd feel lonely. The idea of joining a group tour never appealed to me, so when Brad and Joanne suggested I come along with them on a jaunt to the Orient, I was overjoyed. Not for a single moment did I ever feel like a fifth wheel or a drag because they made me feel so accepted."

A brother speaks of his brother-in-law: "My kid sister, Frankie, used to go out with such a bunch of jerks that when Milt came along we all felt she had struck a gold mine—although he had no money then. And it's twenty-five years since they got married and I still feel the same way about him."

"I never had a sister," Carol, a happily married housewife and mother of three, states, "but if I had ever been able to choose one I'd have chosen Abby, my brother Doug's wife."

A young grandmother confessed to me how her husband's sister actually saved her marriage. During the Viet Nam war, while her husband was overseas for nearly two years, she had been sexually attracted to a young surgeon who worked in the hospital where she was a nurse's aide, and had an affair with him. Loving her husband, nevertheless, she was torn by her conflict and confided in her sister-in-law (her husband's sister) that she felt so guilty she thought she ought to write her husband and tell him about the affair. The sister urged her not to tell because she knew that her brother would be heartbroken. She knew her brother was totally committed to this marriage and that the news might seriously damage it. She also knew that this affair was only temporary, which it was. The wife did not tell her husband about her interlude, and, ending her story, said, "As soon as Jack returned from Nam, I realized how much I loved him. I was so glad that I hadn't hurt him and was forever grateful to Josie."

More than this, in times of serious trouble, or when a death occurs in the family, loved and loving sisters- and brothers-in-law give emotional support and comfort to the family and often take a major part in handling the difficult but necessary arrangements of funerals and burials, etc.

When they have been close and a divorce takes place, the blood sisters or brothers, sorry as they may be, knowing or not knowing all the circumstances that have caused the break, are inclined to rally to the side of their sib. "My older brother, Harry, a sociologist, who is strong for marriage and the family stood right by me during my two divorces," says a thirty-eight-year-old sculptor with pride. "He saw the insoluble problems. My first husband, Jim, was a skirt-chaser, and Jerry—whom he really liked—and I were married just two years when Jerry decided he wanted to give up living in the East and live in Seattle where he would raise cattle. He never considered my wishes, nor did he care that my career was just beginning to take hold and I was being noticed here. No compromises were in order as far as he was concerned. Annie, Herb's wife, was also a prop for me at that time."

With tongue-in-cheek, one brother observed, "Husbands and wives may come and go but brothers and sisters go on forever."

Following a divorce, sometimes a sister- or brother-in-law remains good friends with her or his "ex," particularly if they happened to have been friends before the marriage, although a "nasty" divorce makes this difficult, too.

We can't, however, ignore seedier aspects of the in-law sibling relationship. A sister-in-law or brother-in-law may be thoroughly disliked. "She's beneath us," some will say, or "His family is so vulgar." "That sure is an interfering and overpowering bitch," says another. A sister or brother may see that their sibling is being "led by the nose" by the spouse, who is contentedly unaware of the situation. (The family may not realize that their sister or brother unconsciously needs and enjoys "being led by the nose.") The spouse may be jealous of the wife or husband's attachment to her or his sibling and feel "left out" when they are together. Such married partners may object to hearing about "that evening when we all took a dip in the lake without our clothes on, and got such a bawling out from Mom and Pop," or, they may resent (or be bored) at any such "remember whens" that excluded them, or they may dislike having to listen to old family jokes. These resentments may be merely a dim recognition of their own failed (or missed) sibling relationships, each one unaware that their failures or the failures of their sisters and brothers were not all of their making, but more likely a consequence of their own lonely, unheard, or unanswered cry for help, tenderness, or love from unhearing parents.

A sister or brother may see a spouse's opposite-sex sib as a rival. One only child, after her marriage, became angry and testy every spring when her husband went off on a fishing trip with his sister, an adventure they had shared since adolescence. Yet, when asked to join, she flatly refused.

No discussion on in-law relationships is complete without some words from Dr. Evelyn M. Duvall's famous study, *In-Laws: Pro and Con.* Dr. Duvall says that sisters-in-law are considered as the "Number Two hazard in number of complaints and in the experience of most people, mothers-in-law being first. Sisters-in-law come in four different varieties. The woman's sister-in-law can be her brother's wife, her husband's sister; a man can have a sister-in-law in his wife's sister or his brother's wife. Generally speaking, it seems that the most troublesome sister-in-law is the sister of the husband."

In Dr. Duvall's study, sisters-in-law have been known to be unfriendly, cold, nonaccepting, critical, smug, self-righteous, boastful, gossipy, possessive, and demanding. Some show "tendencies to meddle, criticize, to be dependent, to be possessive, to pamper and to intrude. . . . These sisters-in-law seem to have the same difficulty as their mothers in letting their brothers go. They find it hard to share their beloved male with another woman—his wife. They persist in being mother figure of the more objectionable type." Dr. Duvall also sees that some of the other sister-in-law problems caused by "competitiveness, rivalry, tattling, boasting, etc.," seem to have their origins in the earlier brother-sister relationships in childhood that were fraught with sibling rivalry. "As patterns of bickering, comparing, and belittling continue onto adulthood, the spouses of the competing siblings are drawn into the quibbling orbit, much to their reported distress."

Brothers-in-law seem to escape with the least amount of flak, although they, too, come in for criticism. A common wisecrack among businessmen is "If you run into an idiot in an important executive position, it is probably the brother-in-law of the president."

Dr. Duvall's summary of brothers-in-law points out that the most frequent sentiments expressed are that he is "incompetent and irresponsible," "somewhat dependent on his relatives," and "thoughtlessly inconsiderate and unappreciative in his relationships with them."

Brothers-in-law who were considered to be dominating of their younger brother in childhood repeated these patterns even after their younger brother married, Dr. Duvall points out. Such an attitude is found to be objectionable in the eyes of the wife of the younger brother who sees her brother-in-law as "self-righteous, interfering, and critical."[4]

The relationship between sisters and brothers runs the gamut from deep love and friendship to bitter hostility and rancor. Attitudes that develop in childhood can continue to operate for the good or bad in the sister- and brother-in-law relationships later in marriage. The early relationships formed between sisters and brothers do not *always* change for the better, and sometimes the early jealousies and resentments or domineering tendencies may carry over and spoil the relationships with sibs-in-law. But here is the Greek chorus repeating again, "All this needn't be the end of the world." When things go awry, some fresh insights into the whys and wherefores of these carryovers from childhood experiences might help the old and new families to get a firmer footing on the road to a happier future.

Complementary Marriages

Dr. Walter Toman, professor of psychology at the University of Erlangen-Nurnberg, has some interesting theories about marriage and a couple's birth order. After conducting many studies, including one in Germany on 2,300 families, Dr. Toman believes that marriages are the most compatible when the partner is married to someone whose sibling position is "complementary." This means being married to someone who is the middle child that you may have been, or, if you were the elder sister of a brother, and married a brother who had an elder sister, and so on. Dr. Toman found that siblings who came from families of mixed sexes have a better chance of happiness in marriage because they are accustomed to living with someone of the opposite sex.

Not so long ago Dr. Toman gave a paper on this subject at the Topeka Psychoanalytic Society, "Dynamics of Family Constellation: Their Contribution to Psychoanalysis." In summing up this paper for *The Bulletin of the Menninger Clinic,* Dr. Ann Applebaum reports, "By contrast, a marriage between a man who is the older brother of a brother and a woman who is the older sister of a sister would be exceptionally difficult since neither is accustomed to a life with a peer of the opposite sex and both will be competing for leadership." Concerning the 2,300 families Toman studied, the *Bulletin* says, "Of the hundred couples that had been married for more than ten years, thirty-one had complementary relationships, while only eighteen of one hundred divorced couples did." Dr. Toman also found that the highest divorce rates were among only children, most likely, he observed, because the single child "needs to be a star, the major focus of the partner's attention and interest."[5]

These findings shouldn't be taken too literally. Only children do not always need or want to be stars. In fact, Dr. Murray Kappelman, pediatrician and an only child himself, writes, in *Raising the Only Child,* "The ability to have the other person so close after long years of aloneness often makes the only child an eager, caring, almost overly solicitous mate."[6] And couples needn't fly at each other during fights with, "It's all because you're an older brother of a younger brother and you think you can boss me like you bossed him, but let me tell you, I am an older sister of sisters and *can't* be bossed!" Nor need a couple contemplating marriage stop and wonder whether they should call the whole thing off because their sibling positions don't match. Other facts—both past and present, conscious and unconscious—go into marital conflict or incompatibility. However, by being aware that position in the family order and all its childhood hangovers can *also* bear an imprint in their mutual reactions and behavior, wives and husbands may be able to straighten out some of their problems with added insight.

Aunts and Uncles

Today there is much talk about the need for "connectedness," for family reunions, of people's desire to trace their family roots. In whatever is left of the extended family of former days, the atmosphere of love—where it exists—cannot help but rub off on the younger members, and their fights with each are more often than not just surface ones. Just as we sensed and reacted as children to the emotional climate in our homes as warm or cold, so we learned what kinship meant as we listened to our parents talk about their own sisters and brothers. Happy responses between adult aunts and uncles stimulated further happy responses between us and our siblings. That very special feeling of "belonging" to a family of aunts and uncles who may have remembered our birthdays with a card, or phone call, or gift as a token of their interest and affection, may have fostered our own feelings of warmth and loyalty to them. "How we loved to look at the family album showing how Uncle Joe, Aunt Edith, and Uncle Bob looked when they were six and eight and fourteen," muses a brain surgeon from Canada, who now has inherited the albums he intends to hand down to his children.

Get-togethers may be rare if the aunts and uncles live some distance away. Gatherings may take place only on birthdays or holidays or on special occasions, but they matter, nonetheless. Cousins with whom to share experiences and compare notes add to the excitement even though these occasions are not always sweetness and light and may include some outbursts or wrangling between the cousins, a part of the warp and woof of childhood living.

At these celebrations—or at more frequent ones when these aunts and uncles live nearby—some disagreement or controversy is bound to come up since people never see things eye to eye all of the time. But arguments can occur without nastiness or hurt. Differences of opinion do not lessen feelings of love. "Sure," a father told his two children, "I used to scrap a lot with Uncle Joe in the same way as you do with Ken, but see what great friends we are now even though we don't always agree?"

It is not always so positive. "Huh!" said a young graduate student in philosophy. "Our aunts and uncles don't even know we're alive and if they did they couldn't care less." Others grumble that their aunts are so competitive that "it trickles down to us cousins who become the objects and victims of their rivalry and we find ourselves, unwittingly, competitors, too."

Lillian Hellman gives still another grim picture in *An Unfinished Woman*, as she describes the forceful impact of great-aunts and uncles on her mother's side. Some who have not admired members of their parents' or grandparents' generation may identify with her words. "Then there were the Sunday dinners with great-uncles and aunts sometimes in attendance, full of open ill will about who had the most money, or who spent it too lavishly, who would inherit what, which had bought what rug that would last forever. . . ." But Hellman adored her father's two unmarried sisters who "were free, generous, and funny," and of whom she writes lovingly.[7]

Many sisters and brothers—forming a unity through their common dislike—vow they'll never be like one of their aunts or uncles. Yet everyone knows of a caring aunt or uncle, who has tried to give the other members of the family a boost in some way. Such aunts and uncles may send or help to send nieces and nephews through college, for example, while refusing to let them feel beholden to them. Or they may help to give them an introduction to key persons in their chosen careers or work, opening doors that otherwise might have been closed.

Some aunts and uncles give much of themselves in other ways to their nieces and nephews, giving them comfort in times of trouble, teaching them a hobby, sharing opinions with them, and generally taking a real interest in their lives. Stories are legion of aunts and uncles adopting children when one or both parents has died. "Families are *made* to stretch," says an aunt in Jane Howard's book *Families,* who rushes off with her husband to Los Angeles to return with and adopt "their suddenly orphaned nieces."[8]

A childless aunt sums it up this way: "My brother's children are to me as my very own, and I consider *their* children as my grandchildren. I had it made because I never had the responsibilities of their upbringing and their day-to-day problems but could always look forward to their comings and goings, which we mutually relished."

15

Illness and Loss of Sibling and Parent

The brother's eyes began to fill with tears at the mention of his younger sister's name whose death had occurred two years ago when she was forty-five. But he refused to discuss either his sister or her death, and his face hardened again.

When sisters and brothers are able to face their feelings, to weep and mourn the loss of their sibling at the time of the death—without "keeping it all in"—the healing process moves just a little faster. If the sorrow is held within, that person may remain depressed for some time, or become melancholy. We have heard people say, "She never got over his loss." Part of these reactions have to do with guilt and the attendant unconscious need for self-punishment.

Loss and Guilt

A freakish and tragic water accident occurred when the motor boat driven by Gwen, age twenty, was run into by an approaching speedboat. The approach was so sudden and rapid that Gwen was unable to alter her course, and as her younger brother, Tod, was thrown into the water, his head struck the side of one of the boats and he was killed instantly. Gwen could not be convinced that this accident was not her fault. After her initial hysterics, Gwen seemed to freeze, showing no emotion at all. A psychiatrist was brought in. He knew that along with her real sorrow over the loss of her adored brother, Gwen was suffering from "survivor guilt," a reaction that sets in sometimes when one person survives an accident fatal to another or others. This happens frequently in wartime when a soldier's buddy is killed before his eyes. The surviving soldier is relieved that his life was spared, yet experiences overwhelming guilt because of his relief and because it wasn't he who died. The conflict can become so great that a person becomes paralyzed; he cannot walk, hear, see, etc. These symptoms are functional, or psychological, not organic, which means there is physically nothing wrong with the man or woman as determined by tests. It is only through intense psychotherapy that such a paralysis can disappear, because the paralysis is an unconscious form of self-punishment.

Gwen was convinced that she should have been able to save her brother somehow. Her inability to feel was another kind of paralysis—of the emotions—and some of these reactions were connected with the normal ambivalent feelings she had had toward her brother in childhood and even as an adult.

When in childhood a sister or brother in the family has a prolonged illness, becomes seriously ill, has an accident or illness resulting in a permanent handicap, some of these same guilt feelings may emerge. Aside from genuine sympathy and fears for this loved and afflicted sister or brother, the siblings may feel envious and resentful of all the anxious attention given the sick child, particularly if for the time being their own needs are somewhat neglected. While they are worried about their sibling, the others may feel ashamed and guilty over their angry thoughts. Sometimes the sisters and brothers fear down deep that if Janey or Willie got that sickness, they too might succumb to it. Or they may have sinking feelings such as, "I was mean not to have let Bobby use my roller skates that time." As the children remember past fights they feel they shouldn't have punched, kicked, or bitten Freddy or Sarah, or have called them bad names. Children's anger may even make them secretly wish for the complete obliteration of a sister or brother. To make matters even worse, young children often imagine that their thoughts have magic power and can cause a calamity. And they have no way of knowing that their sibling may have held the same mean thoughts about them. These often deeply buried thoughts may reappear later in life during an adult sister or brother's illness, or death.

In the event of the death of a sister or brother, among adults as well as children, the survivor may be tormented with the feeling that she or he should have been a better brother or sister. Even when we have apparently been the most devoted wife or husband, sister or brother, it is almost inevitable that we should feel that somehow we could have done more. We regret those impatient, angry, critical, or neglectful moments, not pausing to recall all the good times we had together. "I should have taken that trip to visit my sister in England," a dress designer laments. "We were such close sisters in childhood and we hadn't seen each other in five years. I promised every year that I'd come over, and it would have been easier for me to do the traveling because of her financial difficulties. But there was always some reason for which I had to postpone the trip, and one day she keeled over with a heart attack and was gone. I'll never forgive myself for my neglect."

Similar thoughts evidently troubled Antoine de Saint-Exupéry, the celebrated French aviator and author of *The Little Prince*. In July 1944 Saint-Exupéry took off from Corsica on a reconnaissance mission from which he never returned, nor was any trace ever found of him or of his plane.

In a psychoanalytic study of Saint-Exupéry, Dr. Bernard C. Meyer calls attention to the fact that the flyer was not only depressed from time to time throughout his life, but had been involved in a seemingly "endless parade of accidents," resulting in serious injuries, due in part to his well-known carelessness and absent-mindedness. Some believed he "courted death." Seeking to account for these events, Dr. Meyer notes that Saint-Exupéry had lost his father when he was four years old under circumstances that were evidently unclear to the boy. Little mourning took place in the household and the event seems to have been blocked out of Antoine's memory. Later, when he was seventeen, his younger brother, Francois, died of rheumatic heart disease. For several years thereafter "the course of Antoine's life appears uncertain and aimless," writes Dr. Meyer. He was moody and depressed, and in his writings he depicted "haunting images of sick and dying children"—similar to the scene of the death of the Little Prince.

Meyer believes that Saint-Exupéry suffered from a persistent sense of guilt toward his brother Francois, which expressed itself in self-destructive behavior. As a child he had tyrannized his brother, and on one occasion he became hysterical when, during some roughhousing Francois injured his head and bled profusely. In Dr. Meyer's opinion the death of the brother, moreover, rekindled some latent psychological conflicts associated with the early and unexplained loss of the father.[1]

Fifty-year-old Agatha still remembers the day when she was nine and had a nasty fight with her sister, Mary, five years older. As she went off to school she yelled at her, "Drop *dead!*" "Upon my return from school later that afternoon," she recalls, "I was told that Mary was in the hospital, about to have an operation. I guess I was too upset to understand that she had 'acute appendicitis' but I was sure that Mary was going to die and that I would have been the cause of her death. I prayed and promised I'd never ever say anything bad to Mary again if she lived." Her sister recovered rapidly.

Several months later, children being children (and adults being adults) of course she "forgot" her vows.

Children may also feel unconsciously that *they* deserve to be punished because of their mean thoughts or actions. They fear also that they will succumb to the same illness or death of their sister or brother as part of the punishment. Adults may no longer be conscious of these tortuous conflicts, but under circumstances involving the health of a loved one, these feelings may rise to the surface in passing moments and cause further anguish and worry.

"I cried out at night and had terrible nightmares when I was eight," Leonard, now a busy pediatrician, says of an early experience. His younger brother, Chip, developed a tumor behind his eye, which, although successfully removed through an operation, caused the boy the loss of that eye. "I loved Chip and wanted to stay with him all the time and not play with the gang. Dad, always sensitive and knowing, sensed that my unhappiness went deeper. He reassured me that any fights I had had with Chip or names I had called him were not responsible for his predicament. He gave me sufficient reassurance so that when Chip was well again we all treated him as we had before. Mother and Dad would not let Chip feel like a handicapped child or treat him as one, which also meant much for his own mental health as well as ours."

The death of a sister or brother can be a disturbing reminder to a child that life holds some mysterious danger; he or she might also be taken away from parents and home. Children may display open grief similar to an adult's, or the grief may be so hidden that they seem apathetic or refuse to mention it. Although discussions and feelings cannot be forced, sometimes as the family recalls happy memories shared together with its lost member, the child may begin to talk about the sibling too.

Occasionally, and unwittingly, sometimes, after their own grief has subsided, parents enshrine their lost child—of any age—in their memory, idealizing that child as one who was so exceptionally "good," "considerate and thoughtful," or "outstanding." The remaining sibling, whether eight, eighteen, or twenty-eight may find it hard to live up to this glorified—and false—version of someone he or she knew so well, and may resent the dead sister or brother, which will lead to guilt feelings.

Emotional responses to the death of an adult sister or brother may also depend to a large degree on the age of the deceased as well as the age of the surviving siblings. Naturally, losing a sister or brother who is in the prime of life is significantly different from losing an aged sibling, but the pain is there, nonetheless. Furthermore, the responses may be affected by whether the siblings had been living apart for many years with little or no contact with one another through reunions, letters, or talks on the telephone, or whether they had kept in touch, keeping their connections alive. And a sudden death will be more of a shock than a long drawn-out illness that would have given the sister or brother more time to be prepared and to adjust in *some* measure to the loss.

There are other factors, too. People's ability to cope with loss is related to the way in which they were helped (or not) to master earlier bereavements in childhood. Sisters or brothers may not have been able to come to terms with an earlier death of a parent or sibling, possibly because the parents themselves were sometimes so overcome by the death that they could not be there in spirit to help the bewildered children understand what was happening. Or they shut out the child from the event, believing in all good will that they were "protecting" him from suffering. Frightening fantasies were often far more upsetting to the child than being told the truth. Sharing in the sad but palliative ceremony of a funeral that joins all the family together in sorrow helps us to grieve, too, and later in life to avoid running away from our feelings. There is evidence that without such help, and with backgrounds of repression, adults may suffer from a greater sense of grief. In a strange way, the present loss touches on or reawakens unconscious memories of the un-mourned, therefore, the unresolved grief of the earlier loss.

If the pain seems overwhelming to the surviving sib-lings, talking with a religious leader, a counselor, or therapist may help the sisters or brothers work through their anguish. If they are helped to feel their feelings and painful memories —past and present—the pain may fade away gradually, and the sister or brother may better understand that death is a part of life.

Responsibility for Aging Parents

Later in life, when a widowed mother or father becomes ailing or feeble, there may be strong disagreements among the sisters and brothers over who is to take on the largest proportion of responsibility, over whether the parent should be urged to enter a nursing home, over which sister or brother can house the parent, and arguments over countless details of the parent-patient at home or elsewhere. All of these critical decisions can bring to the fore some of the best or worst childhood sibling emotions.

It is not always the eldest who assumes responsibility at such times. Over the years a particular sister or brother may have grown and matured, surprising the others by having stepped out of her or his original role, although sometimes others refuse to recognize the change. For example—as shown earlier—neat as a brother may have become, the oth-ers insist on seeing him as "the slob." Occasionally, "the kid" or "the flibberty-gibbet" may stun the others by coming through during a crisis with a calm and strength no one ever thought possible. One youngest brother of three older sisters admits that he had always been spoiled and considered the baby of the family. Yet when their seventy-five-year-old widowed mother broke her hip, it was he who turned out to be the emotionally supportive member of the family, and its chief adviser. Everyone remarked, admiringly, "Who'd have thought our little Herby would turn out to be the Rock of Gibraltar?"

Or it may be, as Silverstone and Hyman write in their book *You and Your Aging Parents:*

> A highly competitive group of brothers and sisters may continue to compete later in life, although not quite as directly with each other. But when their mother begins to age, they may resume open competition with each other over her welfare, particularly if she was the original source of their competitiveness. Each sibling may claim to be considering Mother's well-being, but the underlying motivation is winning out in a final family contest.[2]

Sisters and brothers once involved in bitter childhood power struggles may now involve their parent in a tug-of-war between them. During such a critical time a sibling may announce, "You were always Mother's favorite; it's up to *you* to look after her now." Or, "You're the eldest, it's *you* who should take care of Dad." Then, too, one sister volunteers to shoulder the responsibility because she feels that here is that last chance to be singled out and appreciated by the parent for all of her "goodness." Or maybe a brother feels that at last *he'll* make it as his parent's favorite ("Maybe Pop will see what a marvelous son I am and change his will in my favor"). Still another may take over the burden because she wants to gain stature in her siblings' eyes and earn *their* respect and recognition. The favorite child may come forth because he or she feels an obligation not only to Mom or Dad, but to his or her less-loved sisters and brothers.

While part of all their motives may be genuine love and generosity of spirit and compassion, this is not always the case, and when it isn't, the care may lack the loving touch an aging parent needs. Sometimes the older children may have married and gone off, leaving the youngest to bear the full brunt of the burden with little concern for either the care-giving sibling's inconvenience or the parent's well-being.

"What a shock," Silverstone and Hyman exclaim, "to discover that your forty-five-year-old sister is just as selfish as ever, or that your sixty-year-old brother is still trying to boss everyone."[3]

In other situations, sisters and brothers may make attempts to settle their early rivalries, inciting each other only further. Sisters and brothers may feel guilty because they are not assuming their share of the responsibility, and to push away their disturbing feelings further pick on the sib who is doing her or his bit to make Mother or Father comfortable, by complaining, "You should have done this or that, or done it in this way or that." Like little children who quarrel, and sulk and cry *"I thought of it first,"* a sister or brother may turn down a plan the other made just because it wasn't her or his idea. "It wasn't *my* idea to dump Mom into that dreary nursing home."

Although it may sound this way, these adults are not unfeeling beasts; they are human like anyone else, and under strain. Furthermore, they may be completely unaware of what is causing their anxiety and hostility, ignorant of the fact that the source of their troubled feelings toward one another goes back a long way.

Under the best and more usual circumstances, brothers and sisters come together from near and far to ask, "How can we all share in this problem, in ways that are best for Dad (or Mom) and in ways that he, too, thinks will be best for him?" Their parent's condition usually brings out feelings of compassion and cooperation rather than conflict. Because they are long free of childhood angers and hostility, or, if there were any, let bygones be bygones, they can calmly and rationally consider all the various courses of action, balancing the needs and interests of all.

Siblings and Loss of the Remaining Parent

When ties between sisters and brothers have been loose, often they disintegrate once the remaining parent—the parent who had kept the family unified—dies.

A prominent family tells of its parting after the death of the mother. Elliott Roosevelt and James Brough write in their book *Mother R: Eleanor Roosevelt's Unfinished Story:*

> We five not-so-young Roosevelts had continued to walk our separate ways, heedless of Mother's yearnings to unite us as a family worthy of her name. There was no trace of kinship. We had broken with each other as we had with her. . . . I knew that we should never meet as a family again.[4]

A forty-year-old librarian told me that when her mother died, her two sisters and brother, all of whom lived at not a great distance, just went their own ways. "The family seemed to fall apart," she says sadly. "Ben, my husband, and I tried to gather Elena, David, and Vicky together for Christmas, and it worked the first year, but somehow the spirit was lacking and the meaning of it all wasn't there any more. The following Christmas Dave and his family begged off because they all wanted to go skiing, and Elena said she didn't think we'd mind if she and her two kids didn't come because she was rehearsing for a new play and couldn't really spare the time. It was rather lonely for Vicky, my youngest sister who had just been divorced, to be without the others. This all couldn't have happened when Mother was alive."

More often than not, the picture isn't so gloomy. When the last parent dies, sisters and brothers renew and strengthen their ties, vowing not to lose touch if they live far apart, and to meet more often if they live nearby, as they did at those family gatherings when their parents were alive.

Sometimes the loss of their parents—their shared grief —helps sisters and brothers forget their petty quarrels, if they had any, and their jealousies, if these remained. Years after, just a knowing look, a nod of the head, an embrace, brings back a flood of memories when the parents are mentioned. Knowing that the loss of kinship as well as parent may leave a deep void not easily filled, siblings often feel a renewed need for one another. Their common link to a former life and the desire to carry on to a degree some of the family traditions remains firm.

16
Money and Property

Bob asked his brother, Edgar, and sister, Rose, to lend him money to keep his failing business afloat. Although Edgar and Rose could easily have afforded the loan, they considered it a poor risk and turned it down. Bob took the refusal as a total rejection of himself and his business ability, and as an indication that they couldn't care less if he failed. The resulting bad feelings lasted for years despite the fact that he got a bank loan and the business was saved.

The Meaning of Money among Siblings

The only son, the youngest, with four older sisters, having become the "man of the family," took care of the family inheritance which was invested in the family business. For years his pleasure in doling out funds in a patriarchal way and the pleasure of his sisters in receiving such proof of his attention through regular receipt of their share kept things on an even keel. No one questioned his right to dispose of funds that belonged equally to them all. When, later, he plunged recklessly into speculations that took a disastrous turn, one sister, the most able, put her foot down. In the ensuing battle the long quiescent nursery rivalries sprang up again. After several years of discord this most competent sister lost out in the battle of who would now become head of the family, because one of the sisters staunchly took the brother's side while the other two shifted uneasily back and forth. Nine years after the calamity, stalemated in her wish to displace her incompetent brother, the strong sister and her brother no longer speak, and the family's finances remain in a precarious position.

When adults continue such a "silent treatment" feud for years, inevitably they have reverted to the angry childhood wishes for revenge when as children they would shout, "I won't play with you any more!" or "I'm never going to speak to you again!" While children may quickly make up and forgive each other, forgetting their recent vows of abandonment, adult sisters and brothers who long to renew contact may be afraid of losing face—that ever troublesome pride again.

A Boston economist tells a story about his mother, aunt, and uncle that combines the worst and best of sibling relationships. "My mother and Aunt Ethel had, ever since I was old enough to notice, the craziest kind of competitive streak between them. They were kind and generous to friends, but when Mother's birthday came around she'd look at her sister's gift and invariably say, 'That stingy bitch, I spent three more dollars on *her* present!' And my cousin Gary, also my age, told me that Aunt Ethel said the very same words when she received *her* birthday present from *my* mother. This competitiveness went so far that at my high school graduation, Aunt Ethel gave me a pair of silver cuff links that had belonged to her husband, Uncle Joel, who had died the previous year. Mother, so furious that her sister hadn't spent any money on me, sent Gary a cheap shoe polishing kit for *his* graduation!" However, the economist told me, his Uncle Danny, the brother of his mother and aunt, had never been able to make ends meet. As a lawyer he had done poorly, so he turned to real estate. But his earnings there barely kept his family going. Without being asked, his mother and Aunt

Ethel decided, generously, to give him a few thousand dollars yearly, as a "supplementary" income. "Uncle Danny," the economist said, "being a man, was not considered competition."

Money as Love

There is always a danger when money is constantly offered to children as bribes, as special rewards, and as punishments.

Frances Loman Feldman wrote years ago in her book *The Family in a Money World:*

> ... The use of money to stimulate performance arouses a variety of feelings in the child. The money he receives assumes unwarranted magnitude since it symbolizes parental acceptance or rejection. It stimulates sibling rivalry and develops demanding attitudes in the child, as he struggles to be the most favored one. He may use it negatively in the relationship with his brothers and sisters to bolster him in his rivalries with them.[1]

As noted earlier, children often equate money and material objects with love. We get things, we are good, we are loved. "If you are good you will get a present, or two dollars." To the child this means approval and love. We don't get things or they are taken away; we are bad and not loved. "If you are naughty you won't get your allowance for two weeks, or that bike for Christmas." To the child this means withdrawal of love. Money can also be used in this way as a tool for manipulating and controlling the child. Later in life, added to the basic issue of love, these other symbols of its value give money matters even more complicated meanings. Money may become the barometer that measures a person's sense of self-worth, power and control over others. It may become a way of gaining prestige over sisters and brothers when strong competitiveness exists among them. There are endless stories of sisters and brothers whose altercations over money divided them for many years—if not forever.

One of two sisters (who are known to be a "living legend" of sisterly love and closeness, both having families and interesting and important careers in somewhat related professions) says that her mother gave them some good advice when they were eight and ten. When they were haggling and fretting over nickels and dimes, this wise woman said, "Don't ever get into fights over money. Those nickels and dimes you are arguing over now may become arguments over much much larger sums of money when you are older, and could split you up for the rest of your lives." The sisters never forgot their mother's words.

When feelings between sisters and brothers are basically sound, money is not apt to come between them. They are not apt to think in terms of, "What's he ever done for me? Why should I help him now?" Instead, sisters and brothers will invariably come to the financial aid of each other when necessary—and not to gain power, not to gain control, not to derive prestige or even engender an obligation.

Family Wills and Favoritism

Even before mourning has ceased, sometimes the reading of a will may reopen the wounds of earlier days when one sibling felt the other child was favored over him or her—and bitterness sets in.

A headline in *The New York Times* financial section some years ago read, "A Will Splits Matarazzo Family of Brazil." In this will the father left control of a holding company he owned, worth a half billion dollars, "in the hands of his daughter, Maria Pia, who was then thirty-three years old and the youngest of five children, including another daughter and three sons." Because this particular child was singled out, two of the brothers have taken legal action against their sister, claiming that she lacked business ability, in order to gain control of the company. The father had written specifically in his will that it represented "no diminution of the great love I always had for my children."[2]

But do heirs always see things this way? No matter how paltry the sums involved, sisters and brothers do *not* always see things this way. Sibling fights over inheritance go back to the beginning of time. For adult children who have not learned that money and love are *not* related—and even at times for those who have—it is impossible sometimes to understand any other "reasons" there should be unequal distribution of money and property. They may deeply resent the sibling who receives "more" (love) no matter what the reality. Relationships between sisters and brothers that have been fragile to begin with can be easily and permanently shattered through legacies.

About one hundred years ago another such will wrought havoc within a family. In 1878 Commodore Cornelius Vanderbilt died at the age of eighty-three, leaving well over one hundred million, then solid, tax-free dollars. He divided the sum unequally among his ten children, because, in this case, they did not please him equally. (Several of his daughters angered him because they disapproved of his marriage at eighty to a woman fifty years his junior.) Five of his daughters received $250,000 outright, and three other daughters were given slightly larger but unequal amounts in trust, the capital to go back into the estate if they had no issue—by-passing their husbands. His disfavored youngest son, Cornelius, Jr., had not inherited a taste for making money (it seemed too futile to him) and he could earn but little when he tried. He frequented brothels and gambling houses, got into debt, and had to borrow money. It was he who received the least share of the estate, in trust and to be returned to the estate upon his death. The funds were to be given to him *only* if his behavior was "exemplary." And this behavior was subject to the approval of his much-loathed brother, William, the family trustee, paragon of virtue and a moneymaker. William, this favorite son, received the remainder of the estate, which, at that time was still more than $100 million. Anger and hatred were rampant among the heirs, and C. V., Jr., and two of his sisters contested the will. The trial created a scandal, during which the family linen was washed publicly. Eventually, some minor settlements were agreed upon. Two years later Cornelius, Jr., once again got into debt, slid further downhill, and shot himself to death.[3]

It may never have occurred to the elder Vanderbilt that the will may have been seen by his heirs as a measure of his love. But his unhappy youngest son must have surely felt this legacy as a direct punishment and further proof of his unworthiness and unlovableness.

Outright and purposeful punishment can be meted out to unfavored children through legacies. Joan Crawford adopted four children: Christina, Christopher, Cathy, and Cynthia. It was Christina, the oldest child, and her brother, Christopher, four years younger, who were singled out for severe physical abuse and humiliations by Crawford (who had been a physically and morally abused child herself). In his book *Joan Crawford*, Bob Thomas states that Crawford knew that she could discipline Christina by "hurting her dignity." To give just a random sample of endless maltreatments and indignities the children suffered, one day when Christina was five, she asked, "Mommy, dearest, don't you think I have beautiful hair?" whereupon Crawford, fearing vanity in her child, picked up a pair of scissors and sheared off her blond hair. Christopher was often locked into closets and, when six, was spanked with bare behind exposed in front of Joan's dinner guests. Thomas writes that housekeepers and governesses told of "relentless beatings . . . over insignificant offenses." The children rebelled. Christopher ran away from home several times in childhood and, in her teens, Christina defied her mother, both thus further inciting their mother's anger.

Crawford remained a vindictive mother toward her eldest children, who "were unable to fill the concept their mother created for them," writes Thomas. In her will she bequeathed her personal property, Thomas says, "to the nearest and most attentive of her daughters, Cathy. To both Cathy and Cindy she left $77,500." There were bequests to others and to charitable organizations. The final blow to her two eldest children was the sentence which read, "It is my intention to make no provision herein for my son Christopher or my daughter Christina for reasons which are well known to them."[4]

Wills not only divide money—even the smallest sums—but can divide families. One will that smacked of the sex favoritism and the lack of confidence traditionally shown about the financial capability of a woman caused a final rupture in the relationship between a sister and brother.

A widow died eight years ago leaving half of her money to her married son who had children, and the other half to her married daughter who was childless and past her childbearing years. However, the childless daughter was given her share in trust—not outright as with her brother (similar in psychological intent as Vanderbilt's legacy, showing how women were thought of in those days)—and with instructions that upon *her* death, the principal would be passed on to her brother's children. Since that day the sister will not speak to her brother, although he has made several attempts to make peace with her over this "offense" not of his doing. An intimate family friend goes into more detail: "Edna [the mother] behaved outrageously. She had always made a big fuss of Harry, pampering him and giving ample proof to others that she thought him more attractive and competent than Ruth. Ruth felt certain, more than ever, that she hadn't been loved as much as her brother because she was a girl. The added proof and insult was the crude indication that her mother thought her disqualified from being able to handle her own money and affairs because she was a female. Didn't her mother know she was capable of knowing how to dispose of her money when she died? Hadn't she seen Ruth's demonstrated and genuine love for her nieces and nephew? Harry, naturally, became the target for all of Ruth's frustrations, angers, and hurts—of the past, and of now."

Sometimes when there has been open communication in a family, parents decide to discuss their intentions before drawing up a will that is unequal. Another widow, wanting to provide fairly for her two grown daughters, saw that her elder one was less secure financially than her younger daughter, whose husband was successful. She thought she would give the older daughter, therefore, a larger share of her modest estate. Hesitant to make a permanent decision, however, she decided to talk things over with her younger child, who quickly pointed out several drawbacks. Sure, her daughter reminded her, her husband was doing well in business and she, too, had a good job as sales manager of a hosiery company. But they might divorce, or lose their job or jobs. More important, she said, "Somewhere, down deep inside of me a voice might always say, 'Maybe Mother really loved Sally more.' "

From these brief vignettes it is easy to see how rivalrous and resentful feelings between sisters and brothers, even quiescent feelings, can be rekindled by disparities in inheritance, and how the one who receives less believes she or he is loved less.

Dividing Family Possessions

Soon after the death of their last parent, daughters and sons have the painful task of emptying a house or apartment filled with their mother's and father's personal and cherished belongings. This heavy task comes all too soon, when tears are barely dry and grief is yet to be worked through. Each personal effect dredges up memories of earlier, happier days. Yet this dividing of things can also set sisters and brothers at each other's throats. Stories are almost legion about siblings who act like little children again, haggling, and yelling at each other, *"I* wanted that clock!" "The bracelet was meant for *me!"* "You always knew that I wanted this figurine for my Emily!"

A brother-in-law describes the behavior of his wife's two sisters and brother when they divided up the contents of their parents' house. "As soon as one of them said he or she wanted something, the other would announce the desire for that object too. It wasn't so much that they wanted the item as that they didn't want the *other* to have it."

Dr. Walter Stewart reminds us, "Most always, these silver candelabras, that antique tea set, or the exquisite brooch are symbols of Mother and her love. If, in your mind, you always felt you had to fight over that love, your fight may continue over the battleground of her treasures. While the sense of loss may be deep, the dissensions over who is to take what also keeps the feeling going that Mother is still alive and you can still fight over her—if you hadn't resolved that need long ago. But all of this is only human, too."[5]

Many sisters and brothers, however, are probably willing to see that the others receive the object that means the most to them—in terms of its association with their parent—and that they choose what they really need and could use, even if one of them needs "more" than the others. Obviously then, they are dividing *things,* not *love.* "You take the chairs, John; you always fancied them and your own set is falling apart." "Go ahead, speak up, we know you always loved great-grandma's portrait, which would look so well on that empty space of your living room wall." If more than one sibling seems to crave a particular memento, these differences are apt to be worked out reasonably (maybe, at times, with some slight, fleeting, childish disappointment or resentment), just as the sibs dealt reasonably with their other problems as they grew up. Strangely, after everything has been disposed of, in a spirit of goodwill, each sister and brother usually gets whatever she or he really wants.

One far-sighted mother of three daughters whom she knew loved the fine paintings, silver, and other family heirlooms of beauty and value in her home enclosed a letter in her will asking the oldest daughter to assemble three equal shares of various articles. Each daughter was then to draw lots for the "bundle" she was to receive. (The same was done with her furniture, with the second daughter in charge, and with jewelry and knick-knacks, with the third daughter making up lots.) Once the parcels were theirs, they could swap things as they wished, free from suspicion that any one of them had been singled out over another.

This mother's exquisite sensitivity not only showed in the way she settled the disposition of her property but in the way she had always handled her three daughters' normal rivalry in childhood.

While the fight over mother's love is usually resolved by adulthood, sometimes it isn't, and, as Dr. Stewart observes, then the material objects come to symbolize mother's love. It is obviously easier to prevent disputes of this order in childhood, and to induce cooperation, than to have to learn sharing later in life in a sad and competitive situation.

Epilogue:
Sisterhood,
Brotherhood

In a number of the contemporary social movements whose goal is the transformation of human relationships from alienation and inferiority to comradeship and a sense of equality, members address each other as "sister" or "brother." In the civil rights movement men and women call each other "brother" and "sister" and may greet each other with special hand clasps of recognition. In the women's movement, sisterhood is a central concept. Both are efforts to establish kinship across family barriers. They define "brother" and "sister" as benevolent terms embodying warmth and caring.

As we have seen, to be a sister and to be a brother can mean a relationship of jealousy and resentment as well as a relationship of love and concern, or hatred without love. But, as with these social movements, when sisterhood and brotherhood are defined as implying equality the meaning is positive not negative.

When sister and brother relationships fall apart, it is not the siblings themselves who are usually the villains but, rather, circumstances and persons backstage in their lives. Those who come to see that they are different but equal— equally loved at home—usually develop a self-esteem essential to loving, tolerance, and the acceptance of an imperfect (as are all mortals) self, and hence an imperfect sibling. Those who receive little such support as children may have been so occupied trying to construct a good self-image that they have had little time to think of others. They may still need to reassure themselves by deprecating their sibling—and, hence, others, in turn.

Is it ever too late to change? We need not conclude that our past failures require future failures. Despite the forgotten childhood promises, the arms twisted, the put-downs, the mean tricks, betrayals, and other injuries suffered at the hands of a sister or brother, a sense of loyalty and affection once dimly felt may still remain beneath the facade of silent or outspoken hostility. Can that younger sister or brother who intruded into our lives but without asking to be born be forgiven? Or can we forgive that older sibling who has bossed us around for years? Some of us continue to wrestle with our conflicting feelings; some of us can forgive and change. Others fail in understanding, and still others do not need to forgive because their love is constant.

In the Bible, Rachel, the more beautiful sister, has the love of her husband, Jacob, but her less-attractive sister, also Jacob's wife, bore him many sons. While Leah hungered for the love of Jacob, childless Rachel yearned despairingly to bear him children. After many years, two sons were born. According to Edith Deen's *All of the Women of the Bible,* Leah and Rachel didn't quarrel openly but "wrestled in mind and spirit through all of their lives."[1]

In Shakespeare's *King Lear,* one sister dispatched the other. After Cordelia was out of the way, her two sisters, Goneril and Regan, began to fight over who would have to take responsibility for their father's care—which neither of them wanted. In the end Goneril poisoned Regan in their jealousy over a man.

Simone de Beauvoir speaks lovingly about her younger sister in *Memoirs of a Dutiful Daughter:* "[Poupette] was my liegeman, my alter ego, my double; we could not do without each other." Later on she reveals more of her closeness to Poupette:

> I owe a great debt to my sister for helping me to externalize many of my dreams in play: she also helped me to rescue my daily life from silence; through her I got into the habit of wanting to communicate with people. . . . When Poupette and I talked together, words had a meaning yet did not weigh too heavily upon us . . . when we were together, we had our own secret garden.[2]

For the director of a small TV station in northern New England a childhood crisis transformed his hostile relationship with his older brother into a loving friendship. "My eleven-year-old brother and I, age eight, had been at constant loggerheads, and, of course, I was always the loser in any physical combats. One day, while playing in the park, I was severely bitten in the leg by a dog. My brother was in anguish over my fright and pain. Mom got a taxi, and during that trip to the doctor Andy held me tenderly to him and tried his best to console and comfort me and give me assurance. Some time after this accident I burst out to my parents, 'I just didn't know until then that Andy really loved me.' "

Strengthening Sibling Bonds

Few families who have shared happy memories—even sad ones—fail to try to keep the desire for connectedness between sisters and brothers and parents alive. Can we ever really break up?

Many families of brothers and sisters cherish their precious bonds and their unity. Festive occasions renew and strengthen their kinship. As Jane Howard writes so vividly in *Families:*

> Good families prize their rituals . . . they evoke a past, imply a future, and hint at continuity. No line in the Seder service at Passover reassures more than the last: "Next year in Jerusalem!" A clan becomes more of a clan each time it gathers to observe a fixed ritual (Christmas, birthdays, Thanksgiving, and so on). . . .[3]

Such occasions give sisters and brothers a chance to validate their mutual view of the world today and as it was in their shared past. A widower in his late fifties, who now lives in Denver, writes, "When you lose a loved companion of many years, and your children, now grown up, have found peers whose lifestyles and values don't always match yours, what a comfort to have brothers and sisters who speak your own language and with whom to share your puzzlement over the generation gap."

While it is true that early patterns and attitudes between siblings may remain quite set, fortunately life itself is open-ended. The very same crisis (illness, a shift in the family's fortune—material or other—the care of an aging parent, or death) that can cause further havoc and grudges can also stimulate close family feeling. A crisis may give sisters and brothers an opportunity to see each other in a different light, and to bury the hatchet once and for all. At such a time—or at less traumatic times after new insight has been gained—we may open up to one another and communicate genuinely for the first time in our lives, or in ways never before possible.

With just one hand reaching out to the other, and listening with open hearts to what the other has to say, sisters and brothers may reveal to one another how many false impressions, misunderstandings, and unintentional hurts have caused their loving feelings of years ago to be plowed under. Once the ground is broken by honesty and acceptance, these good feelings can rise to the surface and bloom again.

"Did you *really* feel this way?", "But *I* thought it was because . . .", "I *never* felt that way about you." One of the great dividends earned from real dialogue may be a different and wiser approach to the younger generation and the sibling problems that may mirror our own. We may see more clearly and personally how our daughters and sons could be affected, just as we were, by our own ancient histories with our families, which can be updated now.

Sisters

No intimate relationship between two human beings who are fairly close in age has a longer, or sometimes more troubled history than that of sister-sister or brother-brother.

Many sisters feel that *their* relationship is the most complex, full of love as well as envy and competitiveness and sometimes even embarrassment over the shortcomings of that closest of all relatives. Along with these conflicting feelings go the attendant guilt and shame for allowing room for such thoughts, some sisters say, because they feel they ought to *love* the other unreservedly. Sister is, after all, their mother or child, or the first female peer they relate to in their lives. If only each sister could realize that the other may feel this same way, each might become more tolerant of her own frailties and not condemn herself. More liberated from guilt and conflict, she may feel freer to love.

Joan Fontaine has written at length of her lifelong feud with her sister, Olivia de Haviland. At the end of her book Joan writes a reproachful but poignant letter to her mother, reminiscing about her childhood. When she and Olivia were young the rules in their childhood home had been strict and unbending, " 'Love one another' was omitted. The milk of human kindness flowed not at all." She writes, "I never knew why you didn't try to make us kinder, more understanding, more forgiving of one another—or did you prefer to see us at each other's throat?"[4] Perhaps here she glimpses the fact that her sister, Olivia, may not have been the real villain in this sibling drama.

Jane Howard wonders whether she and her sister who live in different states would get on as well if they lived next door. "Would we abuse our siblings' right to be less nice to each other than we ever would dare to be to anyone else? Would the laughing rapport which we achieve at our best outbalance regressive snippiness? I rather fear that for us, as for many pairs of siblings, it might not."[5]

Some words of a poem by Sondra Segal in a play, *Sister/Sister,* express what sisters often feel but cannot put into words.

WHY DO I WEEP
A letter to my sister

Why do I weep before I see you?

And after I see you?

Who am I weeping for?

Do I weep for what we've lost
or for what we still bring with us into the present?

Am I saying farewell to something each time I see you?
Is that why I weep?
saying goodbye
to what?
to my child self?
you in childhood?
dead expectations of Mother and Dad?
what I felt you took from me that I can never regain?

What do I weep for?
the family romance
the loss of the family romance
how far I've come away from all of this

Or do I weep at how close it all still is
that every visit with you
my sister
is a visit to the past

to those original family scenes
to powerlessness, competition, unmet need . . .

What do I want from you?
closeness without sameness
support without competition
loyalty without betrayal
an ending to those ancient dualities
an ending to living in comparison

separation without loss

I want to separate from you without losing you

You've been there all along
we've seen the same things
there's no way to say farewell to you
and I've never really wanted to.

and yet
I weep for fear of losing you
the you with whom I seek
a sisterhood of consciousness and friendship

Our relationship is so complex
so laden with the past, with the intensity
    of each of our connections to each of our parents
so laden with the dependency of early childhood, the
    desperation of sibling rivalry, the threat of separation
so full of being torn apart and of being alone . . .

how can we
see one another through all that
see ourselves and one another with consciousness
and with compassion. . . .[6]

Brothers

Some men feel that the conflicts between sisters may have an element of "petty rivalry" or even "catfights," but no relationship, they strongly maintain, can contain such momentary but ferocious feelings of hatred and the wish for revenge as that of brothers. One man illustrates this by pointing to the emotions that spring up when a younger brother is vanquished physically by an older brother, or when the older one is overpowered by a sibling younger than he. Other brothers speak of the equally forceful feelings of loyalty, allegiance, and mutual protection. We have only to think of how Agamemnon came to his younger brother Menelaeus' side to mastermind the Trojan wars after Paris had abducted Menelaeus' beautiful wife, Helen of Troy. And how many of us can recall newspaper accounts of a sibling who risked or lost his life trying to save a brother from drowning, from a fire, or from other accidents?

The Kennedy family's way of life was and is competitive. Rivalry in sports, as in everything else, dominated the clan led by autocrat Joseph Kennedy. He brought his large family up to compete. There was no allowance for defeat. "We don't want any losers around here," he told the children. "In this family we want winners."[7] Yet competition did not lead to antagonisms among these siblings; quite the opposite.

This may well have been because of the genuine love Joseph, but, particularly, Rose Kennedy gave to each son and daughter, including their retarded daughter, Rosemary. Quite likely it was because of this love that a good measure of the competitiveness was channeled into service to the people and mutual help—the daughters into benevolent and religious activities and the sons into politics.

Hank regards compassion as a part of brotherly love. "All my growing years I had wanted to have clout with my eldest brother, Frank, who had made so much of my childhood a misery and who could only think of me as 'that little squirt!' But after I had dreamed for many years of getting even with Frank by making it in the big world some day and saying to him, '*Now* aren't you sorry?' '*Now* you'll appreciate me,' something strange happened to me one day. I had found peace with myself; I was happy with my family. I was doing well at work, which gave me tremendous pleasure. And there was Frank who suddenly appeared so different to me. He, too, had gone through life and suffered in his own way. He, too, was a human being who had needed to prove his own worth. I felt almost cheated out of my revenge at that moment. I no longer wanted it. Instead, a compassionate fellow-feeling took over."

Forgiveness, understanding, compassion. These too are key words. Esau forgave Jacob for the cruel tricks he had played on him many years before. When Jacob knew they would meet again years later, he feared Esau's revenge and hid his family. Instead, Esau ran out to meet his brother, arms outstretched to embrace him. Joseph also finally forgave his brothers for all their treachery—at a time when he was in Egypt and had the power to deny them food, or even to slay them.

It is only from a position of power that lies *within* that true forgiveness, understanding, and compassion are possible. Self-esteem is the barometer for this inner feeling. In having a good sense of self, one can accept one's own humanness, and thereby accept the humanness of others.

Sisterhood-Brotherhood

What do these words really mean? For centuries sisterhood referred primarily to women who belonged to religious and charitable orders and organizations whose main purpose was to further the group with which they were affiliated, or to heal the sick and care for the poor. Sororities brought together women in colleges and professions in common enterprise. A "silent sisterhood" has always existed among women bound together in networks of friendship, love, and mutual support.

But today the word "sisterhood" is not so silent and has a much broader significance. It denotes a feeling of pride among women as they now are helping each other to realize their potential as human beings. It denotes a new tie among women, a bonding together to better the condition of womankind throughout the world. And it suggests that the noncompetitive, mutually reinforcing quest for self-respect of all women—not just some at the expense of others—offers a valuable model for social relationships in a complex world.

Brotherhood also historically has meant a religious order of men, and much more. It has included fraternal groups and societies of all kinds, for good and for evil, gangs as well as men united in good works or a common cause.

"Sisterhood-Brotherhood" describes women and men able to live and work together, transcending sibling or sex rivalry, racial or national identity, looking out for the interest of all human beings.

The emphasis of this book has been on the crying need to raise sisters and brothers as *equal* though *different* human beings, regardless of sex, birth order, or characteristics. Those who know themselves to be equal can become self-respecting adults—reasonably secure, able to find expression for their own needs, and capable of heeding the needs of others. Adults who understand how to deal with the opposing forces within themselves, of love and hate, of competitiveness and sharing, may be more able to enjoy the greater satisfactions of friendliness, affection, and cooperation with their sisters and brothers, wives and husbands. From the small safe community of such a family we can extend these friendly, open, and accepting feelings toward members of the larger community. We may then come nearer to achieving if only in small measure a true Sisterhood and Brotherhood of the world.

Source Notes

Prologue: Understanding the Past, pages 1–6

1. George Santayana with Daniel Cory, *The Life of Reason: Or the Phases of Human Progress,* rev. ed. (New York: Charles Scribner, 1953 [1905]), p. 82.
2. Sigmund Freud, *A General Introduction to Psychoanalysis* (New York: Liveright, 1938), p. 182.
3. Robert W. White, *The Enterprise of Living: Growth and Organization in Personality* (New York: Holt, Rinehart & Winston, 1972), p. 91.

I. SIBLING RIVALRY, SIBLING LOVE

1. Problems of Favoritism, pages 9–23

1. Anne Meredith, *The Sisters* (New York: Random House, 1948), pp. 14, 20.
2. Eugene O'Neill, *Long Day's Journey into Night* (New Haven: Yale University Press, 1956), pp. 165–166.
3. Barbara Silverstone and Helen Kandel Hyman, *You and Your Aging Parents* (New York: Pantheon Books, 1976), pp. 44–45.
4. Barbara Gelb, "A Touch of the Tragic," *New York Times Magazine* (December 11, 1977), pp. 130–132.
5. Dr. Walter A. Stewart, instructor, New York Psychoanalytic Institute, New York City. Personal interview.
6. Saul Bellow, *Humboldt's Gift* (New York: Avon, 1976 [1973]), pp. 169–170.

7. Wyatt Cooper, *Families: A Memoir and a Celebration* (New York: Bantam, 1976 [1975]), pp. 69–70.
8. Simone de Beauvoir, *Memoirs of a Dutiful Daughter* (New York: World Publishing Co., 1957), pp. 45–46.

2. Finding Identity Despite Individual Comparisons, pages 24–33

1. Normal Kiell, *Adolescence in Fiction* (New York: International Universities Press, 1965), p. 177.

3. Competition and Rivalry, pages 34–41

1. Joan Fontaine, *No Bed of Roses* (New York: William Morrow and Company, 1978), pp. 102, 145–146, 188.
2. Wyatt Cooper, *Families: A Memoir and a Celebration* (New York: Bantam, 1976 [1975]), p. 70.

4. Fighting, Teasing, and Solutions, pages 42–52

1. Brian Sutton-Smith and B. G. Rosenberg, *The Sibling* (New York: Holt, Rinehart & Winston, 1970), pp. 40–41.
2. Margaret Drabble, *The Needle's Eye* (New York: Alfred A. Knopf, 1972), p. 344.
3. Sigmund Freud, "On the Psychical Mechanisms of Hysterical Phenomena" (1893), *The Collected Works of Sigmund Freud*, Standard Edition (London: Hogarth Press, 1962), iii, p. 25.
4. Owen Wister, *The Virginian* (New York: Grosset & Dunlap, 1929 [1902]), pp. 28–30.
5. Jessica Mitford, *A Fine Old Conflict* (New York: Alfred A. Knopf, 1977), pp. 10–11.
6. Suzanne Borden-Sandler, "If You Don't Stop Hitting Your Sister, I'm Going to Beat Your Brains Out" (Paper presented at the 83d *Annual Meeting of the American Psychological Association*, Chicago, 1975).

5. Alliances and Cooperation, pages 53–63

1. Stephen Bank and Michael Kahn, "Sisterhood-Brotherhood Is Powerful: Sibling Sub-Systems and Family Therapy," *Family Process* 14:3 (September 1975): 322.

2. James H. S. Bossard and Eleanor Boll, *The Large Family System* (Philadelphia: University of Pennsylvania Press, 1956), p. 153.

3. Ralph Schoenstein, *Yes, My Darling Daughters: Adventures in Fathering* (New York: Farrar, Straus and Giroux, 1976), p. 51.

4. *The 13th Report of the Human Renal Transplant Registry,* ix: 1 (March 1977), American College of Surgeons/National Institutes of Health Organ Transplant Registry, Chicago, Ill. The information on the increase in kidney transplants comes from the End-State Renal Disease Branch, Health Care Financing Administration, Dept. of Health, Education, and Welfare, Baltimore, Maryland.

5. Dr. Milton Viederman, clinical professor of psychiatry, Cornell University Medical Center, New York City. Personal interview.

6. Deena Linett, "Gifts," *Ms.* (March 19, 1978): 67.

6. Siblings and Sex, pages 64–81

1. Dr. Walter A. Stewart, instructer, New York Psychoanalytic Institute, New York City. Personal interview.

2. *Ibid.*

3. Dr. Herman Roiphe, clinical professor of psychiatry, Mount Sinai School of Medicine, New York City. Personal interview.

4. J. D. Salinger, *The Catcher in the Rye* (New York: Signet Books, 1953 [1945]), p. 122.

5. Irene M. Josselyn, *The Happy Child* (New York: Random House, 1955), pp. 338–339.

6. James T. Farrell, *Young Lonigan* (New York: Vanguard Press, 1932), pp. 61–63.

7. Luciano P. R. Santiago, *The Children of Oedipus* (New York: Libra Publishers, 1973), pp. 111–137.

8. Johann Wolfgang von Goethe, *Truth and Poetry from My Own Life,* ed. Parke Goodwin (New York: G. P. Putnam, 1850), Vol. 2, p. 97.

9. Santiago, *Children of Oedipus,* pp. 124–133.

10. John Clive, *Macaulay: The Shaping of the Historian* (New York: Alfred A. Knopf, 1973), pp. 259, 288; Sir George Otto Trevelyan, *The Life and Letters of Lord Macaulay,* in Clive, p. 288.

11. Edmund Lee, *Dorothy Wordsworth: The Story of a Sister's Love* (New York: Dodd, Mead & Co., 1887), pp. 73, 132.

12. Clive, *Macaulay,* pp. 273–274.
13. S. Kirson Weinberg, *Incest Behavior,* rev. ed. (Secaucus, New Jersey, 1976 [1955]), pp. xxi, 41, 45, 59–61, 99, 249, 73–81, 167, 250, 168–170, 254, xvi, 75.
14. Santiago, *Children of Oedipus,* p. 6.

II. BIRTH ORDER

7. Coming First, Then Paradise Lost, pages 85–103

1. Adelina Diamond, "Rosalyn Carter: Her Mother/Herself," *Parents' Magazine* (August 1978): 77.
2. Alfred Adler, *Understanding Human Nature* (New York: Greenberg, 1927), p. 154.
3. Richard L. Zweigenhaft, "Birth Order, Approval-Seeking and Membership in Congress," *Journal of Individual Psychology,* 31:2 (1975): 205–210.
4. Richard D. Lyons, "Study Finds First-Borns Have Higher I.Q.'s," *New York Times* (February 6, 1979): CI-2.
5. *Ibid.*
6. Robert W. White, *The Enterprise of Living: Growth and Organization in Personality* (New York: Holt, Rinehart & Winston, 1972) p. 103.
7. Lucille Forer with Henry Still, *The Birth Order Factor* (New York: David McKay Company, 1976), p. 91.
8. Sigmund Freud, "Constructions in Analysis" (1937), *The Collected Works of Sigmund Freud,* Standard Edition (London: Hogarth Press, 1964), xxiii, p. 261.
9. Joan Fontaine, *No Bed of Roses* (New York: William Morrow and Company, 1978), p. 30.
10. Dr. Walter A. Stewart, instructor, New York Psychoanalytic Institute, New York City. Personal interview.
11. Dr. Sylvia Brody, clinical psychologist and psychoanalyst, Center for Social Research, City University of New York. Personal interview.
12. *Ibid.*
13. Alex Haley, *Roots* (New York: Doubleday & Company, 1976), p. 41.
14. Mopsey Strange Kennedy, "A Last Born Speaks Out at Last," *Newsweek* (November 7, 1977): 23.

8. Secondborn, Coming After, pages 104–112

1. Susan Seliger, "All in the Family," *The Washingtonian* (June 1978): 113.
2. W. Allison Davis and Robert J. Havighurst, *Father of the Man* (Boston: Houghton Mifflin Co., 1947), p. 125.
3. "The Story of the Youth Who Went Forth to Learn What Fear Is" in *Grimm's Fairy Tales* (New York: Pantheon Books, 1944), pp. 29–39; "The Soldier and the King" in *Russian Fairy Tales*, collected by Aleksandr Afanas'ev (New York: Pantheon Books, 1945), pp. 563–567.
4. Bruno Bettelheim, *The Uses of Enchantment: The Meaning and Importance of Fairy Tales* (New York: Vintage Books, 1977 [1976]), pp. 238–239.
5. Mopsey Strange Kennedy, "A Last Born Speaks Out at Last," *Newsweek* (November 7, 1977): 23.

9. Middle Child, the Human Sandwich, pages 113–118

1. Lucille Forer with Henry Still, *The Birth Order Factor* (New York: David McKay Company, 1976), p. 76.
2. Groucho Marx, *Groucho and Me* (New York: Bernard Geis Associates, 1959), p. 32.
3. Joe Adamson, *Groucho, Harpo, Chico—and Sometimes Zeppo* (New York: Simon and Schuster, 1973), p. 27.
4. Arthur Marx, *Son of Groucho* (New York: David Mckay, 1972), p. 175.
5. James H. S. Bossard and Eleanor Boll, *The Large Family System* (Philadelphia: University of Pennsylvania Press, 1956), p. 179.

10. The Youngest, Favorite of Folklore, pages 119–125

1. Brian Sutton-Smith and B. G. Rosenberg, *The Sibling* (New York: Holt, Rinehart & Winston, 1970), p. 3.
2. "The Queen Bee" in *Grimm's Fairy Tales* (New York: Pantheon Books, 1944), pp. 317–319; "The Griffin," pp. 681–688.
3. Bruno Bettelheim, *The Uses of Enchantment* (New York: Vintage Books, 1977 [1976]), p. 103.
4. Charles Baudouin, *The Mind of The Child: A Psychoanalytic Study* (New York: Dodd, Mead and Co., 1933), p. 35.

5. Jane Shapiro, "The Extraordinary Simon Sisters," *Ms.* (February 1977): 53, 84.

11. Twins, the Unique Siblings, pages 126–141

1. Dorothy Burlingham, *Twins: A Study of Three Pairs of Identical Twins* (New York: International Universities Press, 1952), pp. 1–6.
2. Marjorie B. Leonard, "Problems of Identification and Ego Development in Twins," *Psychoanalytic Study of the Child* (New York: International Universities Press, 1961), pp. xvi, 310.
3. Thornton Wilder, *The Bridge of San Luis Rey* (New York: Albert & Charles Boni, 1928), p. 95.
4. Burlingham, *Twins*, p. 87.
5. Herbert Warren Wind, "The Sporting Scene: Centenary," *The New Yorker* (July 25, 1977): 61–64.
6. Wilder, *The Bridge of San Luis Rey*, pp. 95–96.
7. Burlingham, *Twins*, p. 87.
8. "Narcissus," *The New Encyclopedia Brittanica*, 15th ed. (Chicago: Encyclopedia Brittanica, 1974), p. 193.
9. Maeve Brennan, "The Springs of Affection," *The New Yorker* (March 18, 1972): 38–83.

III. SPLITS IN THE FAMILY

12. Broken Homes, pages 145–155

1. Ann S. Kliman, director, Situational Crisis Service, Center for Preventive Psychiatry, White Plains, N.Y. Personal interview.

13. Stepsiblings and Half-Siblings, pages 156–170

1. Lucille Stein, C.S.W., therapist, faculty member of the Bank Street College of Education, and Guidance Counselor, Ethical Culture School in New York City. Personal interview.
2. Anne W. Simon, *Stepchild in the Family: A View of Children in Remarriage* (New York: The Odyssey Press, 1964), p. 202.
3. Edith Atkin and Estelle Rubin, *Part-Time Father* (A Guide for the Divorced Father) (New York: The Vanguard Press, 1976), p. 140.

4. Lucille Duberman, *The Reconstructed Family: A Study of Remarried Couples and Their Children* (Chicago: Nelson-Hall, 1975), p. 73.
5. *Ibid.,* p. 70.
6. Stevanne Auerbach, consultant, Parent and Child Care Resources in San Francisco. Personal interview.
7. Owen and Nancie Spann, *Your Child? I Thought It Was My Child!* (Pasadena, California: Ward Ritchie Press, 1977), p. 143.
8. Paul Bohannan, "Divorce, Chains, Households of Remarriage, and Multiple Divorces," in Paul Bohannan, ed., *Divorce and After* (New York: Doubleday & Company, 1971), pp. 121–122.
9. Lucille Stein. Personal interview.
10. Ann S. Kliman, director, Situational Crisis Service Center for Preventive Psychiatry, White Plains, N.Y. Personal interview.

IV. SPECIAL PROBLEMS OF ADULT BROTHERS AND SISTERS

14. Marriages and the Wider Family, pages 173–185

1. Stephen Bank and Michael Kahn, "Sisterhood-Brotherhood Is Powerful: Sibling Sub-Systems and Family Therapy," *Family Process* 14:3 (September 1975): 325.
2. Louisa M. Alcott, *Little Women* (Boston: Little, Brown, and Company, 1915 [1880]), pp. 253, 292.
3. Margaret Mead, *Blackberry Winter: My Earlier Years* (New York: A Touchstone Book, Simon and Schuster, 1972), p. 70.
4. Evelyn Millis Duvall, *In-Law: Pro and Con* (New York: Association Press, 1954), pp. 221, 241ff., 256ff.
5. Walter Toman, "Dynamics of Family Constellation: Their Contribution to Psychoanalysis," recorded by Dr. Ann Applebaum, *The Bulletin of the Menninger Clinic* 39:6 (1975): 602–607.
6. Murray Kappelman, *Raising the Only Child* (A Signet Book, 1977 [1975]), p. 144.
7. Lillian Hellman, *An Unfinished Woman: A Memoir* (New York: Bantam Books, 1970 [1969]), pp. 2–3.
8. Jane Howard, *Families* (New York: Simon and Schuster, 1978), p. 176.

15. Illness and Loss of Sibling and Parent, pages 186–196

1. Bernard C. Meyer, "The Little Prince: Speculations on the Disappearance of Antoine de Saint-Exupéry," *Journal of the American Psychoanalytic Association* 22:1 (1974).
2. Barbara Silverstone and Helen Kandel Hyman, *You and Your Aging Parents* (New York: Pantheon Books, 1976), p. 43.
3. *Ibid.*, p. 44.
4. Elliott Roosevelt and James Brough, *Mother R: Eleanor Roosevelt's Unfinished Story* (New York: C. P. Putnam's Sons, 1977), p. 279.

16. Money and Property, pages 197–206

1. Frances Loman Feldman, *The Family in a Money World* (New York: Family Service Association of America, 1957), p. 44.
2. David Vidal, "A Will Splits Matarazzo Family of Brazil," *New York Times* (February 20, 1977): D1–D2.
3. Frank Church, "The Commodore Left Two Sons," *American Heritage* (April 1966): 4–8, 81–103.
4. Bob Thomas, *Joan Crawford, A Biography* (New York: Simon and Schuster, 1978), pp. 168–170, 174, 210, 267.
5. Dr. Walter A. Stewart, instructor, New York Psychoanalytic Institute, New York City. Personal interview.

Epilogue: Sisterhood, Brotherhood, pages 207–216

1. Edith Deen, *All of the Women of the Bible* (New York: Harper & Brothers, 1955), pp. 30–33.
2. Simone de Beauvoir, *Memoirs of a Dutiful Daughter* (New York: World Publishing Co., 1957), pp. 46, 47.
3. Jane Howard, *Families* (New York: Simon and Schuster, 1978), p. 270.
4. Joan Fontaine, *No Bed of Roses* (New York: William Morrow and Company, 1978), pp. 302, 304.
5. Jane Howard, *Families,* p. 119.
6. Sondra Segal, "Why Do I Weep, a Letter to My Sister," from the play, *Sister/Sister,* by Claire Coss, Sondra Segal, Roberta Sklar. A production of the Women's Experimental Theater, New York City, 1978.
7. James MacGregor Burns, *Edward Kennedy and the Camelot Legacy* (New York: W. W. Norton, 1976), p. 26.

Further References

Allan, Graham. "Sibling Solidarity." *Journal of Marriage and the Family* 39 (1977):1.

Altus, W. D., "Birth Order and its Sequelae." *Science* 151 (1966):44–49(a).

Arlow, Jacob A. "Fantasy Systems in Twins." *Psychoanalytic Quarterly* 24 (1960):2.

Arnstein, Helene S. *Getting Along with Your Grown-Up* Children. New York: M. Evans and Company, 1970.

———. *What to Tell Your Child About: Birth, Illness, Death, Divorce and Other Family Crises.* rev. ed. New York: Condor Publishing Co. (paper), 1978.

Auerbach, Stevanne. "From Stepparent to Real Parent." *Parents' Magazine* (June 1976).

Bergmann, Thesi, and Wolfe, Sidney. "Observations of the Reactions of Healthy Children to Their Chronically Ill Siblings." *Bulletin of the Philadelphia Association for Psychoanalysis* 21 (1971):3.

Bowerman, Charles E., and Dobash, Rebecca M. "Structural Variations in Intersibling Affect." *Journal of Marriage and the Family* 36 (1974):1.

Bulfinch, Thomas, *Bulfinch's Mythology.* 2nd rev. ed. New York: Thomas Crowell Co., 1970.

Croake, James W., and Hayden, Delbert J. "Trait Oppositeness in Siblings: Test of an Adlerian Tenet." *Journal of Individual Psychology* 30 (1947):2.

Duberman, Lucille. "Stepkin Relationships." *Journal of Marriage and the Family* 35 (1973):2.

225

Einstein, Gertrude, and Moss, Miriam S. "Some Thoughts on Sibling Relationships." *Social Casework* 48 (1967):9.

Feinberg, David. "Preventive Therapy with Siblings of a Dying Child." *Journal of the American Academy of Child Psychiatry* 9 (1970):4.

Fisher, Alfred. "Sibling Relationships with Special Reference to the Problems of the Second Born." *Journal of Pediatrics* 40 (1952).

Flugel, J. C. *The Psychoanalytic Study of the Family.* London: The Hogarth Press, 1966.

Frances, Vera, and Frances, Allen. "The Incest Taboo and Family Structure." *Family Process* 15 (1976):2.

Gedda, Luigi. *Twins in History and Science.* Springfield, Ill.: Charles C. Thomas, 1961.

Glenn, Jules, "Opposite-Sex Twins." *Journal of the American Psychoanalytic Association* 14 (1966):4.

———. "Twins in Disguise." *Psychoanalytic Quarterly* 23 (1974):2.

Harmon, N. B., ed., *The Interpreter's Bible.* Vols. I–IV. New York: Abingdon Press, 1954.

Harris, Irving D. "Birth Order and Responsibility." *Journal of Marriage and the Family* 30 (1968):3.

———. *The Promised Seed: A Comparative Study of Eminent First and Later Sons.* Glencoe, Ill.: Free Press, 1964.

Hawkins, Mary O'Neill. "Jealousy and Rivalry in Brothers and Sisters." *Child Study Magazine* (Summer 1946).

Henry, Jules, and Henry, Zurria. "Symmetrical Reciprocal Hostility in Sibling Rivalry." *American Journal of Orthopsychiatry* 12 (1942):2.

Joseph, Edward D. Report on panel: "The Psychology of Twins." *Journal of the American Psychoanalytic Association* 9 (1961):1.

——— and Tabor, Jack H. "The Simultaneous Analysis of a Pair of Identical Twins and the Twinning Reaction." *Psychoanalytic Study of the Child* 26 (1961).

Juel-Nielsen, Niels, *A Psychological Evaluation of Monozygotic Twins Reared Apart.* Acta Psychiatrica Scandanavica, Supplement, 183. Vol. 40, 1964. Copenhagen: Munksgaard, 1965.

Karpman, Ben. "Psychodynamics in Fraternal Twinship Relations." *Psychoanalytic Review* 1 (1953):40.

Koch, Helen. "The Relation of Certain Formal Attitudes of Siblings to Attitudes Held Toward Each Other and Toward Their Parents." *Monographs of the Society for Research in Child Development* 25 (1960):3, 4.

Larousse Encyclopedia of Mythology. New York: Prometheus Press, 1961.

Lidz, Theodore. *The Person: His Development Through the Life Cycle.* New York: Basic Books, 1969.

Lindon, John A., ed. "A Psychoanalytic View of the Family: A Study of Family Member Interactions." *The Psychoanalytic Forum* 3 (1969).

McArthur, Charles. "Personalities of First and Second Children." *Psychiatry* 19 (1956):1.

Neisser, Edith. *The Eldest Child.* New York: Harper & Brothers, 1957.

Oberndorf, C. P. "Psychoanalysis of Siblings." *American Journal of Psychiatry* 8 (1929):6.

Puner, Helen W. *Helping Brothers and Sisters Get Along* (pamphlet). Prepared in cooperation with the Child Study Association of America. Chicago: Science Research Associates, Inc., 1952.

Rollman-Branch, Hilda S. "The First Born Male Child: Vicissitudes of Pre-Oedipal Problems." *International Journal of Psychoanalysis* 47 (1966):2–3.

Roosevelt, Ruth, and Lofas, Jeannette. *Living in Step.* New York: Stein and Day, 1976.

Rosenbaum, Milton. "Psychological Effects on the Child Raised by an Older Sibling." *American Journal of Orthopsychiatry* 33 (1963):3.

Schulman, Gerda L. "Myths That Intrude on the Adaptation of the Stepfamily." *Social Casework* 53 (1972):3.

Shapiro, Sumner L. "Ever Do in Your Kid Brother?" *Psychiatric Quarterly* 47 (1973):2.

Thomas, Helen. *The Successful Step-parent.* New York: Harper and Row, 1966.

Toman, Walter. *Family Constellation: Theory and Practice of a Psychological Game.* New York: Springer, 1961.

Index

About the Author

A graduate of Sarah Lawrence College, Helene Arnstein worked with several mental health organizations and was affiliated with the Child Study Association of America for twenty-six years, serving terms as a vice-president and long-time Board member. She has written numerous articles on human relations and family life for national magazines including *The Ladies' Home Journal, Family Circle, Parents' Magazine, Family Health,* and the *New York Sunday Times Magazine.* Ms. Arnstein is the author of six previous books; a recent one, *The Roots of Love,* was a winner of the 1975 Family Life Book Award of the Child Study Association of America. She has a grown daughter and son, three young grandchildren, and lives in New York City with her husband.